CLASSIC ROCK CLIMBS
NUMBER 06

HUECO TANKS

by
John Sherman

Chockstone Press
Evergreen, Colorado
1997

Classic Rock Climbs: Hueco Tanks

ISBN: 1-57540-025-1 Classic Rock Climbs series
      1-57540-033-2 Hueco Tanks

All photos by John Sherman.

Published and distributed by
Chockstone Press, Inc.
Post Office Box 3505
Evergreen, CO 80437-3505

TABLE OF CONTENTS

HUECO TANKS STATE PARK

Congratulations! You have just taken the first step to obtaining an intimate addiction to Hueco Tanks climbing. This Classics guide contains over 300 routes and boulder problems, enough to keep you busy for your first few visits. Nevertheless, there are over 250 roped climbs and over 1500 boulder problems in the park. Like any successful pusher, I have given you just enough information to get you hooked on Hueco. Once your fingers taste the delicious syenite, there will be no going back to other winter areas. Every year you will need a Hueco fix. Every year you'll need a bigger dose. Soon you will know that you can't live without the complete Hueco Tanks Climbing and Bouldering Guide by Yours Truly. Hueco Tanks owns you. Chockstone Press owns you...

GETTING THERE Hueco Tanks State Park is located in far West Texas, 32 miles east of El Paso. Most people will approach the area via I-10. The quickest approaches utilize Loop 375, which skirts El Paso to the north and east, avoiding much of the big city traffic. Loop 375 goes by several different names depending which stretch you are on: Trans-Mountain Road, Joe Battle Blvd, or Americas Ave.

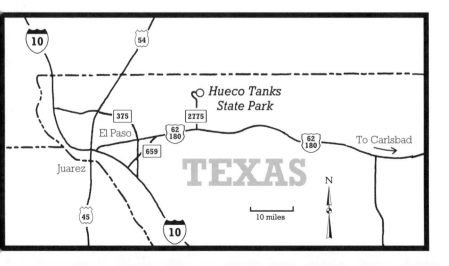

Coming from the north on I-10, take the Trans-Mountain Road exit. Follow Trans-Mountain Road east, over the Franklin Mountains, then through 4 miles of stop lights before it becomes a highway again. Continue on this road for 11 miles to its intersection with 62/180 (AKA Montana Blvd.). At this point, Loop 375 is also called Joe Battle Blvd. Turn left (east) on 62/180 and go 11 miles to the Farm Road 2775 turn off, easily identified by the white "flying saucer" land sales office for Hueco Tanks Estates. Turn north on 2775 (the only way you can turn onto it) and follow it eight miles to the park.

Coming from the south on I-10, take the Americas Ave/Loop 375 exit (exit 34), and turn north on Americas Ave, which is also Loop 375 and soon changes names to become Joe Battle Blvd. Follow this north for 4.6 miles, go through the stop lights at the intersection with Montwood, then in 0.1 mile turn right (northeast) onto Farm Road 659 (AKA Zaragosa Road). Follow 659 for 4.8 miles to its intersection with 62/180. Turn right (east) onto 62/180, then follow it 8 miles to the Farm Road 2775 turnoff described above. Take 2775 eight miles north to the park.

Some people may approach via Alamagordo and US 54. Immediately after crossing the New Mexico/Texas border, turn left onto Dyer St. Follow it south 2.9 miles then turn left onto Railroad Dr. This is the first left turn possible and is marked only by a hazardous cargo route (HC) sign, not by a street name sign. Follow Railroad Drive to its intersection with Loop 375, turn left (east) on 375 and follow it 11 miles to 62/180. From there follow the directions in the I-10-from-the-north scenario above.

If approaching from the east via Carlsbad and 62/180, one must only be alert for the turnoff onto Farm Road 2775 which appears at the bottom of the long descent from the Hueco Mountains.

ENTERING THE PARK As you approach Hueco Tanks from the south, the park appears to be nothing more than a couple of enormous brown lumps. If Paul Bunyon had made it this far south, the lack of trees would be attributed to him and the lumps credited to his ox Babe. Fortunately, Pecos Bill has a lock on the legend stuff around these parts. Don't be put off by initial appearances, the southern aspects of the Hueco rock are usually the least sound. As you drive along the western perimeter of the park the multitude of boulders on the Frontside will be visible, begging you to mount them. First, however, you must get through the entrance station. Recently, the entrance fee structure for the park has changed every year or two. The fees changed once again on May 1, 1996. The revised fees (always subject to change) are as follows:

The daily entry fee is $2.00 per person ages 12 and up. Children under 12 are admitted free. An annual pass, called the Gold Texas Conservation Passport, costs $50.00 and grants unlimited park entry to all Texas State Parks to the member and all passengers traveling in the member's car.

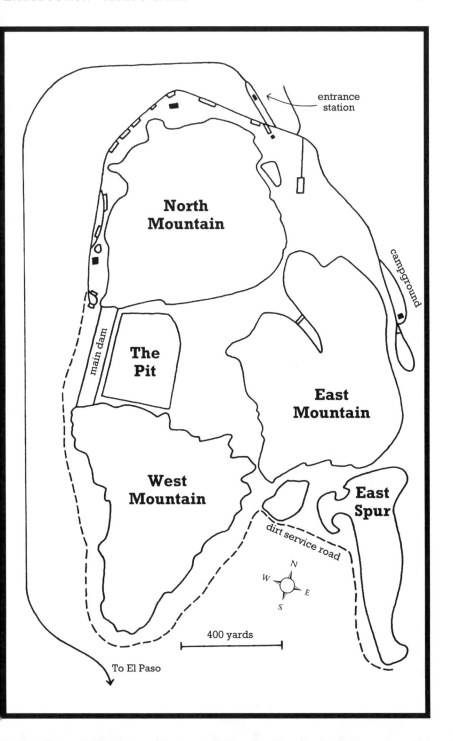

In addition to the entry fee, each person entering the park to go rock climbing or bouldering must pay a climbing activity fee. This fee is $2.00 per person per day. If you have a Conservation Passport, the climbing fee is $1.00 per day for the owner of the passport, and $2.00 per day for each passenger who entered the park in the same vehicle. Each person visiting the park must also fill out a back country permit for each visit, describing which areas the person will be visiting. A single back country permit can be used for a group of people, but only if they stay with each other throughout the day.

If you show up after hours (usually after dark) the gate to the park will be locked. If you have reserved a campsite be sure to call the office during business hours (8 a.m. to 5 p.m.) to get the combination to the gate. The combination changes every Monday.

GENERAL RULES All pets must be on leash at all times. The leash must be attached to a person or a fixed object and may be no longer than 6 feet. The temptation to let Fido run free is hard to resist, but bear in mind that besides terrorizing the native wildlife, dogs have a habit of getting underfoot and seem partial to lounging on sketchpads. I've heard of one dog who was tragically killed by a falling climber this way.

Bicycles are not allowed on the trails or rock slabs in the park; they must remain on paved surfaces at all times.

Do not hop the fence to enter the park.

Public consumption of alcohol is illegal.

CAMPING/ACCOMMODATIONS The campground facilities at Hueco Tanks State Park are outstanding. The heads are heated, the showers are hot, and each site sports electric outlets and a cold water faucet. The 17 standard campsites, with water and electricity currently cost $11.00 per night. You can have up to eight people in the site and two cars. An additional $2.00 parking fee is charged if you have a third vehicle, which must be parked in the overflow lots east of sites 13 and 14. Be sure all wheels of all vehicles are on the pavement or risk the wrath of the rangers. There are three undeveloped sites. They have no electricity and currently cost $8.00 per night.

Campfires are no longer allowed in the park. You must cook on gas or propane stoves (no charcoal).

Quiet hours are 10:00 p.m. to 6 a.m.

During climbing season the campground is nearly always full. To ensure getting a site you should make reservations by calling The Central Reservation Center in Austin: (512) 389-8900 (9 a.m. to 6 p.m. Central Time, Monday through Friday). You can make reservations from 48 hours to 11 months in advance. To guarantee your reservation you must make a deposit equal to one day's fees within five days of making your reservation. Your deposit will be refunded if you cancel your reservation at least 4 days prior to your arrival. To cancel a reservation call (512) 389-8910 (24 hours).

The phone number for Hueco Tanks State Park is (915) 857-1135. *This number will not work for campground reservations; you must call the Austin number above.*

The Hueco Tanks Country Store, AKA Pete's, is the quonset hut located outside the park three miles from the entrance station. You can arrange with Pete to camp outside the hut. When at Pete's, take care not to disturb his neighbor Willy to the north (in the camouflaged compound). Do not park on Willy's property. Respect Willy's privacy.

All of the land surrounding the park is privately owned. If you camp there you will be trespassing and subject to prosecution. Other dangers are angry land owners, coyotes, snakes, rough roads, illegal aliens, and evil dwarfs with chain saws.

OUTSIDE THE PARK The following road log lists the distances from the park entrance station to facilities of interest to climbers, the nearest gas, the nearest food, the cheapest beer, the closest XXX drive in, etc.

Road Log

All distances are in miles from the entrance station along Farm Rd 2775 and 62/180 (aka Montana Boulevard) towards town. N, S refer to north or south side of Montana.

Miles What you'll find

0.0 Nearest Coke machine and public phone – the entrance station

2.9 Nearest food, beer, wine, cafe, pay phone – Hueco Tanks Country Store (Pete's) Hours: around 9AM to 10 PM, but often closed around midday.

13.3 N J & R Supermarket

13.8S Nearest gas – Pete and Bros. (also food, beer, wine, auto mechanic)

14.5S Montana Vista Grocery (and bakery)

14.5N Best Mexican restaurant in East El Paso – El Rancho Escondido

15.2S Sheriff/Fire Dept. (and Papagayo store – gas, food, beer, wine)

15.6S Nearest XXX drive-in – Fiesta drive-in.

21.2S nearest 24 hour gas and ATM (also convenience store) – Diamond Shamrock at George Deiter and Montana.

CLIMBING GEAR Commercial Sales, 520 West San Antonio (downtown) has a very limited, but pricey selection of climbing gear. 542-1721. Pete's sometimes has softwear and chalk for sale.

AT THE PARK

WEATHER AND THE SEASONS West Texas is justifiably famous for its sunshine. It's equally infamous for its winds and dust storms. Rainfall is minimal. El Paso averages about eight inches of precipitation a year, most of it coming in the hot summer months.

Hueco Tanks' reputation is as a winter area and there is no other U.S. area with better climbing and better weather in the winter. Despite all the sunshine, winter can be cold. There are usually two or three days each winter when it snows. Hueco Tanks is over 4000 feet in elevation. Nevertheless, a pleasant day of bouldering can be had if one stays out of the wind and close to the sun. The rock here warms up quickly. At night, temperatures can drop drastically. A 40 degree difference between daily high and low temperatures is common. Bring a good sleeping bag.

The combination of high elevation and desert sunshine can wreak havoc on human skin. Imagine crimson blisters raising on your forehead, leaking thin, clear pus into your eyes. Don't forget sunscreen, lip balm, and a sombrero. Drink lots of water; dehydration can transform tendons from healthy kevlar licorice whips into fragile candy canes.

The most popular months to visit Hueco Tanks are November through March. October and April are also good, but hot for some folks' tastes (70's and 80's). May can be boulderable as well, if one avoids the heat of midday. In June, temperatures hit the triple digits and conditions remain prohibitively hot through September. Only the hardiest locals brave the summer heat.

RANGER RICK TALK Hueco Tanks bustles with biology, from the two dimensional bunnies adorning Farm Road 2775 to freshwater shrimp in the intermittently water-filled huecos atop the mountains. Most of the fauna is well hidden, however, the flora is unavoidable. Nearly all of the plants have spines, hooks, or thorns. Below I've ranked the plants in order from those you'd least like to fall into to those you can walk through with relative impunity.

Heinous	Jingus	Casual
Cactus	Sotol	Cresosote
Mesquite	Goathead burrs	Oak tree
Catclaw	Ocotillo	Lichen
Banana yucca	Most grasses	Ferns
Lechuguilla		

It's worth learning to identify these, not just to avoid them, but also to locate the boulder problems (some problems are located by marker plants, e.g. starts just right of then traverses left over the bloodstained yucca.) See the cartoon at right.

Hueco Tanks is an oasis in an otherwise harsh desert environment. Removal of vegetation from climbs, landings, trails, campsites, etc. is forbidden. When possible, stick to established trails or walk on rock slabs.

As far as fauna goes, the things to look out for are snakes, mosquitoes and scorpions. Rattlers hibernate in the chilly months when conditions are best for climbing. The mosquitoes also disappear at this time. Scorpions hide under rocks, so be careful when you're removing a cheater stone left by some thoughtless climber. Kick it over first before you slide your fingers under it. Scorpions also like to cozy up in shoes. If your shoes smell like mine and you leave them outside the tent at night, be sure to shake them out before you slip the digits in.

ROCK ART Due to the presence of water and game at Hueco Tanks, the area has attracted humans for over 10,000 years. Since pre-historic times, people have left their mark on Hueco Tanks in the form of pictographs (rock paintings). Over 3000 pictographs adorn the walls of Hueco Tanks (not including 20th century graffiti), making the park one of the great rock art sites in North America. The different styles of paintings-the Archaic, the Jornada Mogollon, and the Historic (Apache)-are described in the booklet "Rock paintings At Hueco Tanks State Historical Park," available at the entrance station. This booklet is recommended reading for all visitors to Hueco Tanks. A knowledge of the park's history, both cultural and natural, adds greatly to one's enjoyment of the park. If one looks at Hueco Tanks and sees only an enormous climbing gym, they are missing out big time. Take care not to touch any paintings when viewing them or climbing near them. Learn to recognize the paintings, sometimes only a faded brush stroke or two, so you can avoid touching them.

Several areas in the park are closed to climbing. These are not included in this guide. They are listed in the entrance station and also marked by signs on the rock. The signs show a rappeler overlain by a diagonal "not allowed" bar. Do not climb in these areas.

Remember, Hueco Tanks is a State Archaeological Landmark. If in doubt whether the climb or boulder problem you wish to attempt might adversely affect the park's archaeology, pick another climb; there are more than 1000 in the park to choose from. Have fun.

CLIMBING IN THE PARK

HOW TO USE THIS BOOK   Numbered routes are shown on a topo or photograph. The topos are organized in counterclockwise order around each mountain with side trips up approach paths to boulders above ground level. The lead climb descriptions follow the same order. Use the maps at the beginning of each chapter and follow the dashed approach lines and sequential page numbers around the mountains.

If you're confused finding north, remember that the large earthen Main Dam between North and West Mountains runs north-south.

Unfortunately, many problems can be identified by the graffiti next to them. Graffiti is given in quotation marks; for example "AC/DC Rules" or "Peter loves Muffy."

TOPROPES, BAD LANDINGS, LOOSE ROCK AND SCARY PROBLEMS   Many of the boulder problems at Hueco Tanks have landings a yogi couldn't sleep on. If you fall on a problem listed as having a bad landing, expect to get hurt. Even if the problem isn't listed as having a bad landing, you may still get hurt if you fall and land poorly. Use your judgement; if you're short on that, use a rope.

Just because a boulder problem isn't listed as loose doesn't mean the holds on it will never break. The problems listed as loose are ones on which a climber must pull on hollow sounding holds or carefully avoid them. Solid sounding holds, especially thin ironrock flakes, have been known to snap at Hueco Tanks. This is more often a problem on climbs with few ascents than on the established classics. Beware when attempting what you might think is a first ascent.

The rock at Hueco Tanks becomes friable when wet; allow the rock to dry for 24 hours after it rains before pulling on any flakes. Ninety percent of the holds that break on established problems do so the day after a rain. If you must climb the day after a storm, stick to problems that never get wet in the first place. *Looseness is mentioned only for boulder problems; expect loose holds on most leads of any length at Hueco Tanks.*

Any boulder problem listed as scary is one that I was scared on when climbing it. Anyway, it's my personal opinion, nobody else's, printed here for what benefit it might offer the user. No judgement is printed as to the scariness of lead climbs in this book.

The heights of problems given in the text are distances climbed on a given problem, this is not always the same as the height of the lip. For example, if a problem traverses ten feet before going straight up another fifteen feet, then it is listed as 25' long, although the lip may only be fifteen feet up.

V RATINGS The V rating system is an open ended system for grading boulder problems. Whether a problem is intimidating, scary, loose, or has a bad landing has no effect on the V grade – only the physical difficulty counts – that is, the technicality of the moves combined with the demands on one's power and endurance. Therefore the rating would remain the same whether it was toproped or bouldered. Hence, a scary V2 may be more difficult for some to boulder than a safe V5. It may be tougher to do a V6 without beta than a V7 with the moves shown to you. The ratings are a consensus of opinions of expert boulderers in excellent shape, or when lacking a consensus, the opinion of the first ascensionist and/or author. Abbreviations

BL bad landing

SD sitdown start

TR toprope problem

YOSEMITE DECIMAL RATINGS These are so standardized in the U.S. now as to need no explanation. At Hueco Tanks the postscripts R and X mean the following: R – a fall will result in serious injury, X – a fall will end your climbing career, if not your life.

CHALK White chalk is the only chalk currently legal at Hueco Tanks State Park. Colored chalk was found to stain the rock. Not that white chalk looks any better, but the El Paso Climber's Club does wash the boulders several times a year in agreement with the State Parks.

TICK MARKS Tick marks are chalk lines, dots, arrows, crosshairs, bullseyes, etc. drawn on the rock to point out holds. In the last year couple of season's Hueco climbers have done a commendable job of reducing their reliance on these unsightly "rookie stripes." Let's hope this trend of relying on one's own problem-solving abilities and attunement to the stone continues.

If you absolutely can't see a hold without ticking it, make your marks subtly. Don't draw with a block of chalk. Instead leave a faint thumbprint. Your eyes will be drawn to the hold just as well. Brush the marks off when you're done. When you come upon tick marks, brush them off. It's a small price to pay to climb here.

ROSIN NO POF. POF VERBOTEN. Rosin use is prohibited at Hueco Tanks and is unwelcome anywhere else in the United States.

DOCTORED HOLDS A doctored hold is the signature of a coward. If you can't do a problem with the holds Mother Nature provided, then you're in over your head and don't belong on the problem. Furthermore, Doctoring of holds is considered defacement of the rock, just as spray painting is, and could lead to the park being closed to climbing.

International Rating Systems Compared

German	YDS	British	Australian	French
	5.0			
	5.1			
	5.2			
	5.3			
	5.4			
	5.5			
	5.6			
5+	5.7	4b / VS		5a
6-	5.8	4c	15	5b
6	5.9	HVS	16 / 17	5b / 5c
6+	5.10a	5a	18	5c / 6a
7-	5.10b	E1	19	6a+
7	5.10c	5b	20	6b
7+	5.10d	E2	21	6b+
	5.11a	5c		6c
8-	5.11b	E3	22	6c
8	5.11c		23	6c+
8+	5.11d	6a / E4	24	7a
9-	5.12a		25	7a+
9	5.12b		26	7b
	5.12c	6b / E5	27	7b+
9+	5.12d		28	7c
10-	5.13a	6c / E6		7c+
10	5.13b	7a	29	8a
	5.13c		30	8a+
10+	5.13d	E7	31	8b
11-	5.14a		32	8b+

UNCOMMON SENSE Hueco Tanks is a state historical park. The park's primary mission is to preserve the historical and natural resources of the park. Recreational use is secondary. In other words, Hueco Tanks is not an amusement park created for climbers.

As climbers, we share the park with other user groups such as bird watchers and picnickers. We also share it with each other as climbers. If we wish to retain the privilege of climbing at Hueco Tanks we must show each other respect. Maybe the bird watchers would rather listen to a songbird than to your Dokken CD. How would you like it if they cranked Donny and Marie at volume ten?

Get a clue, don't leave your carpets or sketchpads fixed out in the park. Selfish climbers have gotten the park closed to climbing before, they can do it again. If you find fixed rugs, remove them. They might get YOU and every other climber kicked out of the park. Ditto with picking up tape wads, butts, and chalk and Powerbar wrappers.

The plains clothes officers patrolling the park won't hassle you if you respect the environment, respect others, and keep your nose clean.

PRIOR TO LIFT OFF Before getting on any boulder problem, be sure to locate the descent. Next check the landing for potential hazards in case you fall. If it looks bad take out a life insurance policy and/or recruit a spotter. Step back if you can to check out the holds, lots of jugs turn into sloping butter dishes when you do this. Some huecos might contain broken glass, courtesy of would be Nolan Ryans. Don't wait until you're up there to find this out. Try to pre-visualize a sequence of moves that will get you to the top. Clean the hand and foot holds if necessary and wipe the dirt off your boots. Take the natural aggressiveness that society tries to suppress and cut it loose. Feel the adrenaline jolt through your chest. Let the spittle foam through your lips. Promise yourself you won't let go then...
Crank It!

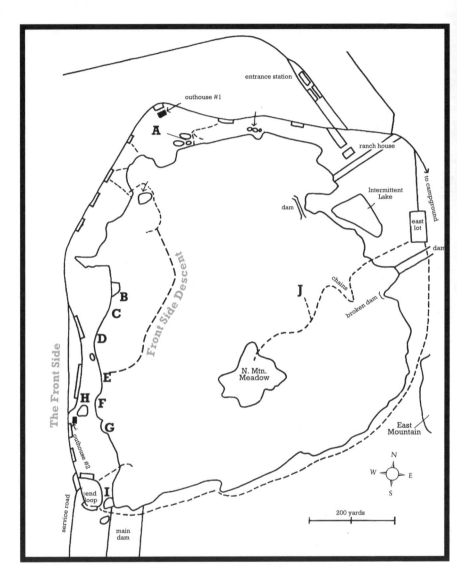

NORTH MOUNTAIN CLIMBING AREAS DIRECTORY

NO.	NAME	PAGE
A	Warm Up Boulder	
B	Flake Roof	
C	Cake Walk	
D	Central Wall	
E	Uriah's Heap	

F	Indecent Exposure Buttress
G	Fox Tower
H	Mushroom Boulder
I	End Loop Boulder
J	Gymnasium

CHAPTER 1

NORTH MOUNTAIN

WARM UP BOULDER

The Warm Up Boulder is located 70 yards southeast of outhouse #1, behind a tree 5 yards southwest of table #6. It is not obvious from the road, being obscured by a tree and the prominent, 40-foot tall Outhouse Rock. This popular boulder gets the morning sun.

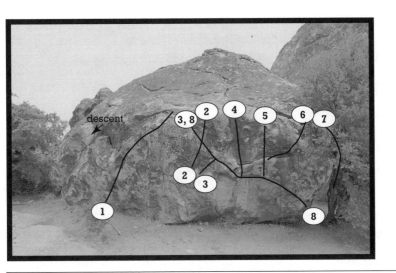

WARM UP BOULDER

1 Namedropper 18 feet V3 SD	5 The Butter Dish 14 feet V2 ★★
2 Murray Lunge 15 feet V6 ★★	6 Big Shot 15 feet V0+ ★
3 Barnstormer 16 feet V1 ★★	7 Noh Bada Wid It 16 feet V0+
4 Thunderbird 15 feet V1 ★★	8 Pounding System 25 feet V4 SD ★★

WARM UP BOULDER
9   Stinking Jesus 17 feet V6 ★★
10 Winking Jesus 14 feet V7 ★

1   **Namedropper 18 feet V3 SD** Sit down start from an incut 3 feet right of "JLB" and 3 feet above the ground. Traverse up and right along the lipline topping out 3 feet left of "Bob, Ethel, Gladys and Ralph."

2   **Murray Lunge 15 feet V6** ★★ Fout feet right of "Harry R. Barnes" is a good flake. Lunge from this 5 feet up to the flake straight above. Everything right of the starter flake is off-route.

3   **Barnstormer 16 feet V1** ★★ Start on the Murray Lunge flake. Zig right then zag left along the flake line to the top.

4   **Thunderbird 15 feet V1** ★★ Climb the crack up the shallow corner. The V1 standard.

5   **The Butter Dish 14 feet V2** ★★

6   **Big Shot 15 feet V0+** ★

7   **Noh Bada Wid It 16 feet V0+** Climb the prow through the branches.

8   **Pounding System 25 feet V4 SD** ★★ Start sitting down behind the tree on the northeast face. Traverse left around the corner, undercling the arch, then finish up Barnstormer.

9   **Stinking Jesus 17 feet V6** ★★

10 **Winking Jesus 14 feet V7** ★ Find "The Burnett Party" graffiti at 8 foot level. A polished scoop 1 foot right of this is on route. Everything else on the polished prow and to its right is off route. Work up sharp flakes above the "Burnett Party" to the top.

THE FRONT SIDE

B	Flake Roof Area		F	Indecent Exposure Buttress
C	Cakewalk Wall		G	Fox Tower
D	Central Wall		H	Mushroom Boulder
E	Uriah's Heap		I	End Loop

THE FRONT SIDE

The Front Side is the imposing west face of North Mountain which extends from the south end of Laguna Prieta to the Fox Tower. It includes The Flake Roof Area, Cakewalk Wall, The Central Wall, Indecent Exposure Buttress (aka Main Buttress) and Fox Tower. Most of the Front Side climbs are from 200 to 350 feet long and don't get sun until almost noon. Great bouldering lines the base of the Front Side.

THE FRONT SIDE DESCENT

The map on the next page of the Front Side Descent is for routes from Cakewalk Wall to Indecent Exposure (Main) Buttress. Descending from Cakewalk Wall is trickier than from the other Front Side routes and involves either a very exposed 3rd or 4th class climbing across a natural chockstone bridge (many climbers will rope up for this), a balls-out one-chance-only jump across the same gap, or a short rappel into the gully below and 2nd class slabs out of the gully. All other Front Side descents should involve few or no 3rd class moves. If you find yourself downclimbing more than one or two moves, you are not on the best route. For routes from All the Nasties to Pink Adrenaline, walk along the top of the Main Wall until atop the route Desperado (marked by the Super Bowl - a 40-foot-wide, 20-foot-deep pit on top of the wall). Then walk east until across a 20-yard wide grassy gully. Head

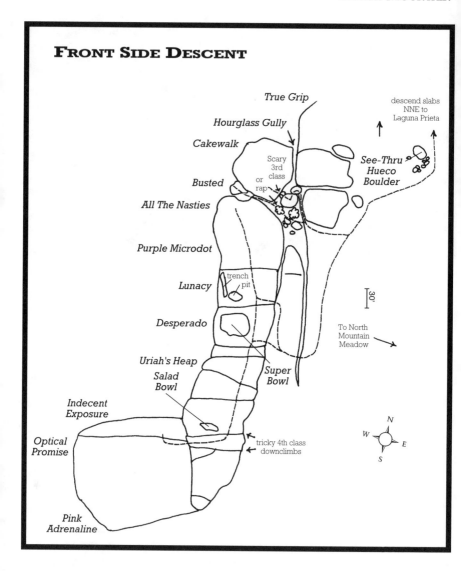

FRONT SIDE DESCENT

True Grip

descend slabs
NNE to
Laguna Prieta

Hourglass Gully

Cakewalk

Scary
3rd
class
or
rap

See-Thru
Hueco
Boulder

Busted

All The Nasties

Purple Microdot

trench
pit

Lunacy

30'

Desperado

To North
Mountain
Meadow

Uriah's Heap

Salad
Bowl

Super
Bowl

Indecent
Exposure

N

Optical
Promise

tricky 4th class
downclimbs

W   E

S

Pink
Adrenaline

*north walking parallel to the gully on its east side until large boulders force
you to the right. From here pass the See-Thru Hueco Boulder (a 17-foot tall
boulder with a 5-inch diameter hole eroded completely through the small
overhang 5 feet below the top) on its right then head north-northeast down
slabs to Laguna Prieta at ground level. Forty feet above ground level a short
3rd class section may be encountered.*

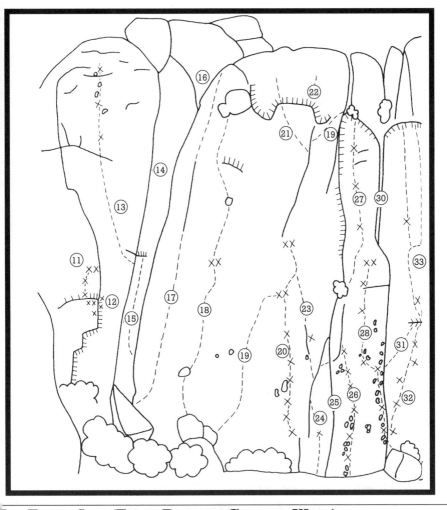

THE FRONT SIDE (FLAKE ROOF TO CENTRAL WALL)

1	Flake Roof 55 feet 5.11 ★★★
2	Flake Roof Indirect 55 feet 5.11– ★
3	True Grip 180 feet 5.10– ★★
4	Left Side 200 feet 5.6
5	Center 200 feet 5.7 X
6	Right Side 200 feet 5.6
7	Son of Cakewalk 250 feet 5.6
8	Return of Cakewalk 280 feet 5.7 ★
9	Cakewalk 300 feet 5.6 ★★★
10	Cakewalk Direct 100 feet 5.9 ★
11	Let Them Eat Cake 20 feet 5.10 R
12	Peasant's Revolt 30 feet 5.8 ★

23	Banana Cake 300 feet 5.10 R
24	Banana Patch 300 feet 5.10 ★
25	Bitchin Chimney 300 feet 5.9
26	Alice In Banana Land 105 feet 5.10– ★
27	Busted 300 feet 5.9 ★
28	Malice in Bucket Land 125 feet 5.9- ★
29	Cowboyography 140 feet 5.13 ★★★
	(not shown on topo–on wall left of Paul Bunyon)
30	Paul Bunyon Chimney 275 feet 5.7
31	All The Nasty Urinals 260 feet 5.9 R
32	Divine Wind 100 feet 5.7
33	All The Nasties 260 feet 5.10 ★★

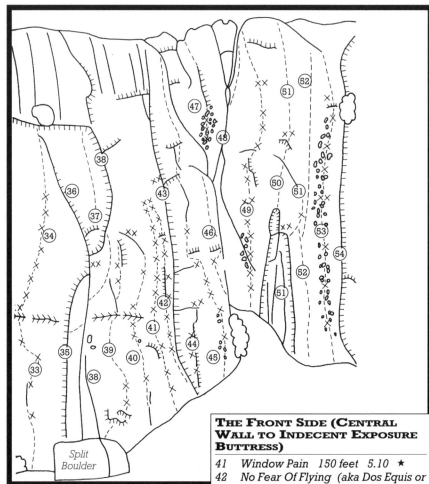

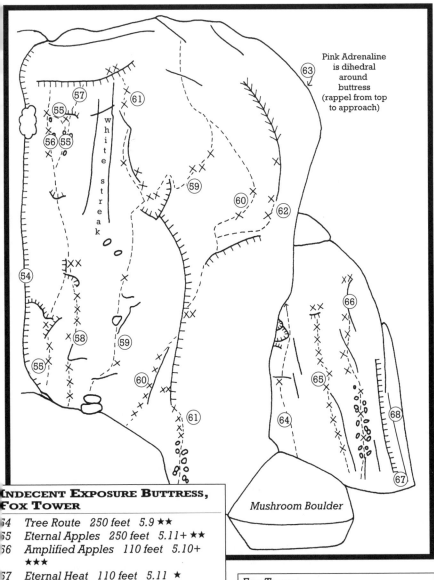

Pink Adrenaline is dihedral around buttress (rappel from top to approach)

w
h
i
t
e

s
t
r
e
a
k

Mushroom Boulder

INDECENT EXPOSURE BUTTRESS, FOX TOWER

54 Tree Route   250 feet   5.9 ★★
55 Eternal Apples   250 feet   5.11+ ★★
56 Amplified Apples   110 feet   5.10+ ★★★
57 Eternal Heat   110 feet   5.11 ★
58 Amplified Heat   260 feet   5.11+ ★★
59 Indecent Exposure   300 feet   5.9+ ★★★
60 Rainbow Bridge   330 feet   5.11 R ★★★
61 Deliverance   350 feet   5.12– ★★
62 Optical Promise   350 feet   5.11+ ★★★
63 Pink Adrenaline   140 feet   5.11+ ★★★

Fox Tower
64 Buttless Goulies   200 feet   5.10 X
65 Head Fox   150 feet   5.10 ★★
66 Fox Trot   165 feet   5.9+ ★★
67 Fox Tower Indirect   200 feet 5.9
68 Fox Tower   200 feet   5.8

MUSHROOM BOULDER

The Mushroom Boulder is the huge rock north of Outhouse #2. The North Face is perhaps the best single bouldering face in the United States. To descend, scramble down the west side.

Problems 69-73 are on the South Face.

69   **Family Size 14 feet V0**   ★

70   **Busted 15 feet V0+** ★

71   **Legal High 19 feet V0+** ★

72   **Twisted 19 feet V3** ★

73   **Hueco Cranks 29 feet 5.12 TR** ★★★

74   **New Chautauqua 40 feet 5.10+** ★   Begin 4 feet right of the southeast corner of the Mushroom Boulder. Climb past 3 bolts then move right into a dihedral. Climb to a bolt, then left out of the dihedral to the top. Toprope variation: 5.11– Instead of moving right into the dihedral, continue straight up the face.

75   **The East Arête 25 feet 5.9**   The two bolt arête on the left edge of the east face.

76   **East Face 20-25 feet V0** ★★ **BL**   Numerous lines have been bouldered up the face right of The East Arête.

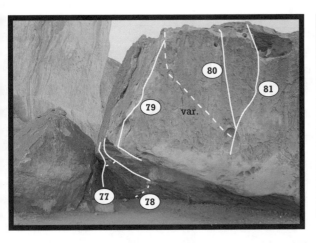

NORTH FACE OF THE MUSHROOM

77	*That's Entertainment 18 feet V6 ★★*
78	*Mushroom Roof 18 feet V8 ★★★*
79	*Crap Arête (aka Dynamo Hum) 18 feet V4*
80	*Left El Sherman (aka What's Left Of Les Left) 18 feet V4 ★★*
81	*What's Left of Les (aka Right El Sherman) 18 feet V2 ★★★*

77 That's Entertainment 18 feet V6 ★★ SD Start sitting in the sand next to a small rock between two small boulders on the east side of the Mushroom Boulder. The hands are at the 3 foot level at the left most incut of a series of incut overlaps that trend right under the gap between Satellite 3 (the northwestern of the two small boulders) and the Mushroom. 8 feet left and slightly up of this starting incut, Holgar Woltrand inscribed his name. Traverse the incuts right under the gap, being sure not to touch Satellite 3. After making it through the gap, conquer the lip at your first convenience. Bad landing in spots.

78 Mushroom Roof 18 feet V8 ★★★ Start on the 9-inch thick hueco pitted flake at the back of the roof. Climb flakes out the roof topping out either left or right. This problem has also been started on the far left end of the hueco pitted flake, adding 8 feet of butt-dragging moves and increasing the pump at the lip.

NORTH FACE OF THE MUSHROOM BOULDER

79 Crap Arête (aka Dynamo Hum) 18 feet V4

80 Left El Sherman (aka What's Left Of Les Left) 18 feet V4 ★★
Variation: Traverse left from the big hole to the Crap Arête (V5).

81 What's Left of Les (aka Right El Sherman) 18 feet V2 ★★★

82 Stuck Inside of Baltimore (aka Left El Murray) 17 feet V6 ★★★

83 Texas Medicine (aka Center El Murray) 17 feet V6 ★★★

84 Railroad Gin (aka Right El Murray) 17 feet V8 ★★★
Numerous variations have been done on the El Murrays. Four of the more significant follow:

Variation 1: The sit down start to the Left and Center routes is a three-star classic. V7 either way.

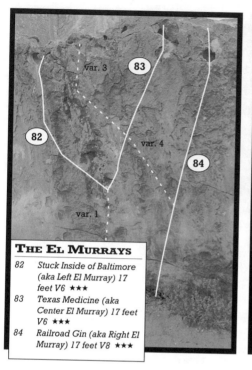

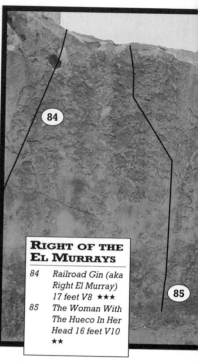

THE EL MURRAYS

82 *Stuck Inside of Baltimore (aka Left El Murray) 17 feet V6* ★★★

83 *Texas Medicine (aka Center El Murray) 17 feet V6* ★★★

84 *Railroad Gin (aka Right El Murray) 17 feet V8* ★★★

RIGHT OF THE EL MURRAYS

84 *Railroad Gin (aka Right El Murray) 17 feet V8* ★★★

85 *The Woman With The Hueco In Her Head 16 feet V10* ★★

Variation 2: Double lunge from the start of Center El Murray to the "inverted-V hold" 12 feet up. Murray's way.

Variation 3: Climb the Center route to the "inverted V hold" then finish between the Left and Center routes (V7).

Variation 4: Start on Right El Murray, finish on Center (V7).

85 **The Woman With The Hueco In Her Head 16 feet V10** ★★

86 **My Fifteen Minutes 15 feet V7** ★ Variation: **Microdick 27 feet V8** ★★ Starts between the Wannabes, traverse left to My Fifteen Minutes and finish up that.

87 **The Local Flakes 14 feet V2** ★★

88 **Local Flakes Direct 24 feet V4** ★ Up and left to The Local Flakes top out. The right angling flake on The Local Flakes is off-route. The upper holds are on.

89 **Micropope 15 feet V8** ★★ Climb the wall between The Local Flakes direct and Left Wannabe. The left foot uses holds on Local Flakes Direct which are off-route for the hands. All other holds used are exclusively on Micropope.

90 **Left Wannabe 15 feet V0+** ★★

91 **Right Wannabe 15 feet V0+** ★★

END LOOP BOULDER

At the end loop of the Front Side road is a huge boulder with two popular 30-foot toprope climbs on its north face; this is End Loop Boulder.

92 **Wyoming Cowgirl 35 feet 5.12– ★★ TR** Top rope the face 11 feet to the left of the crack on the northwest face. This has also been led. Variations exist on either side of this line: to the left 5.11+, to the right 5.12.

93 **The End 30 feet 5.10 TR**

94 **Back Side 30 feet 5.12 TR ★**

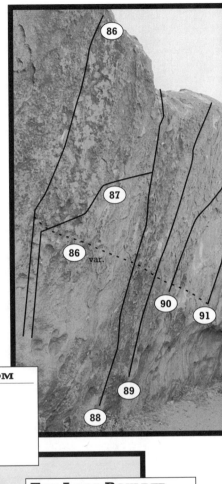

NORTH FACE OF THE MUSHROOM

86	*My Fifteen Minutes 15 feet V7* ★
87	*The Local Flakes 14 feet V2* ★★
88	*Local Flakes Direct 24 feet V4* ★
89	*Micropope 15 feet V8* ★★
90	*Left Wannabe 15 feet V0+* ★★
91	*Right Wannabe 15 feet V0+* ★★

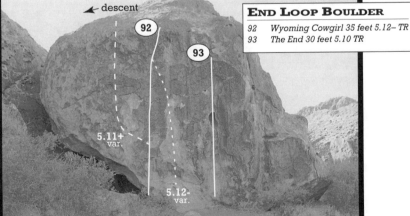

END LOOP BOULDER

92	*Wyoming Cowgirl 35 feet 5.12– TR*
93	*The End 30 feet 5.10 TR*

THE GYMNASIUM

The Gymnasium is one of the most classic bouldering walls at Hueco Tanks. It is also one of the coldest. To find it walk 70 yards southwest from the top of the chains. For 35 yards a 25-30 foot cliff line will be on your right split by several cracks. This is the Chain Wall. After 35 yards you will encounter lots of 10-15 foot high boulders, the Small Potatoes. Walk through these, under some, keeping the main rock bodies to your right. After squeaking past the last potato you should see a small tree, lots of cactus and a 40 foot hand to fist crack (Entrance Crack, 5.10) splits the east face of the main rocks next to the entrance to a chimney. Scramble through this chimney. After 35 feet it opens up to form the Gymnasium. The last squeeze through the chimney can be avoided by staying high to the east and dropping in midway along the wall. Midway along the overhanging wall is a prominent black water streak descending from a notch. Descend down the tree next to the water streak or off the northwest end of the wall.

NORTH MOUNTAIN SEEN FROM EAST PARKING LOT

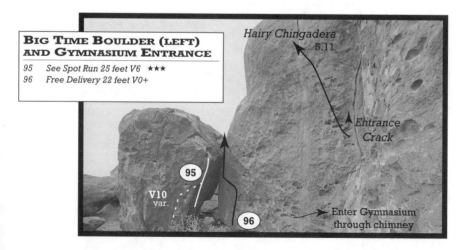

BIG TIME BOULDER (LEFT) AND GYMNASIUM ENTRANCE

95   *See Spot Run 25 feet V6* ★★★
96   *Free Delivery 22 feet V0+*

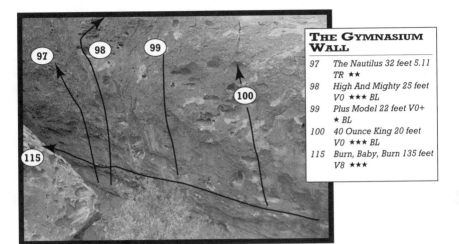

THE GYMNASIUM WALL

97 The Nautilus 32 feet 5.11 TR ★★
98 High And Mighty 25 feet V0 ★★★ BL
99 Plus Model 22 feet V0+ ★ BL
100 40 Ounce King 20 feet V0 ★★★ BL
115 Burn, Baby, Burn 135 feet V8 ★★★

THE GYMNASIUM WALL

97 **The Nautilus 32 feet 5.11 TR** ★★ Climb the wall 5 feet left of High And Mighty, finishing up a left angling thin crack at the top.

98 **High And Mighty 25 feet V0** ★★★ **BL** Move right at the end for an easier top out. Don't fall.

99 **Plus Model 22 feet V0+ ★ BL**

100 **40 Ounce King 20 feet V0** ★★★ **BL** Start left, right, or directly to reach this line.

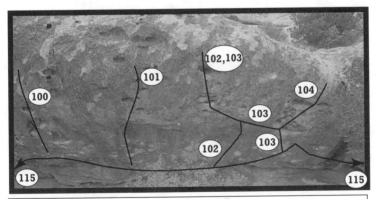

THE GYMNASIUM WALL – LEFT SIDE

100 40 Ounce King 20 feet V0 ★★★ BL
101 Suck In Dick 22 feet V6 ★★
102 The William's Throw 22 feet V5 ★★
103 Punk Funk 29 feet V2 ★★★

104 Bad Axe 17 feet V ★
115 Burn, Baby, Burn 135 feet V8 ★★★

THE GYMNASIUM WALL — CENTER

105 Rhymes With Rich 12 feet V3 ★
106 Only The Little People Pay Taxes 12 feet V3 ★
107 Gag Reflex 12 feet V2 ★
108 Solid Pleasure 15 feet V0 ★★
109 World Without Lawyers 16 feet V0 ★★
110 Jimmy Hats On Parade 16 feet V0 ★★
115 Burn, Baby, Burn 135 feet V8 ★★★

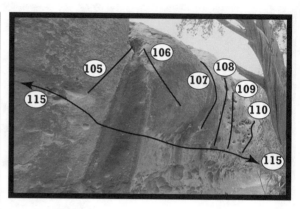

101 Suck In Dick 22 feet V6 ★★

102 The William's Throw 22 feet V5 ★★

103 Punk Funk 29 feet V2 ★★★

104 Bad Axe 17 feet V1 ★ scary

105 Rhymes With Rich 12 feet V3 ★

106 Only The Little People Pay Taxes 12 feet V3 ★

107 Gag Reflex 12 feet V2 ★

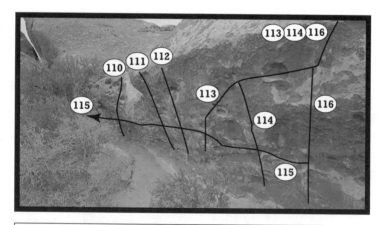

THE GYMNASIUM WALL — RIGHT SIDE

110 Jimmy Hats On Parade 16 feet V0 ★★
111 The Belly Bomber 19 feet V1 ★
112 Bellyful Of Marrow Pudding 20 feet V1 ★
113 Continuous Discriminating Entertainment 29 feet V1 ★
114 On A Bender 20 feet V1 ★
115 Burn, Baby, Burn 135 feet V8 ★★★
116 Leapin Lizards 18 feet V5 ★

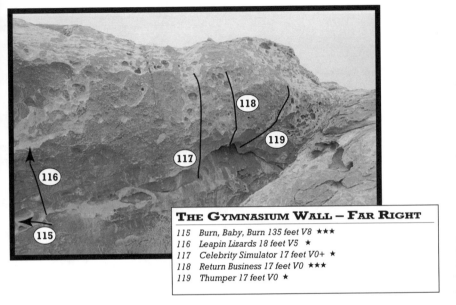

THE GYMNASIUM WALL — FAR RIGHT

115 Burn, Baby, Burn 135 feet V8 ★★★
116 Leapin Lizards 18 feet V5 ★
117 Celebrity Simulator 17 feet V0+ ★
118 Return Business 17 feet V0 ★★★
119 Thumper 17 feet V0 ★

108 **Solid Pleasure 15 feet V0** ★★ The wall 10 feet right of the waterstreak. A small tree is just behind it.

109 **World Without Lawyers 16 feet V0** ★★ 13 feet right of the waterstreak.

110 **Jimmy Hats On Parade 16 feet V0** ★★

111 **The Belly Bomber 19 feet V1** ★ scary, loose

112 **Bellyful Of Marrow Pudding 20 feet V1** ★ scary

113 **Continuous Discriminating Entertainment 29 feet V1** ★

114 **On A Bender 20 feet V1** ★

115 **Burn, Baby, Burn 135 feet V8** ★★★ Starting 2 feet right of the faded peace sign, traverse the wall from right to left, eliminating the slabby foot holds low down and the top of the waterstreak. It ends with both hands on a smile shaped jug 6 feet before the wall turns to a squeeze chimney at it's far left end. Pumper.

116 **Leapin Lizards 18 feet V5** ★ scary Some loose holds.

117 **Celebrity Simulator 17 feet V0+** ★

118 **Return Business 17 feet V0** ★★★

119 **Thumper 17 feet V0** ★

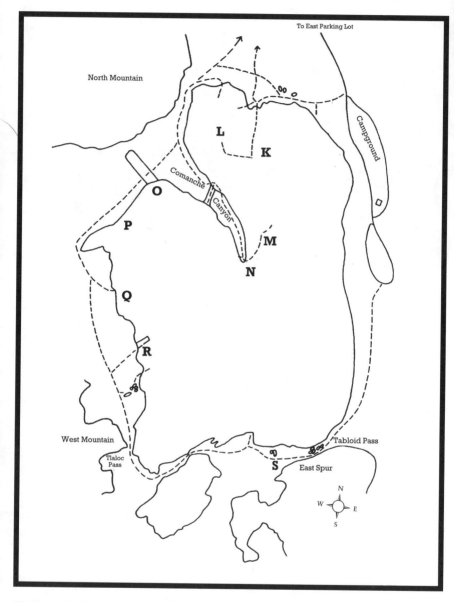

EAST MOUNTAIN CLIMBING AREAS DIRECTORY

K   Dragon's Den
L   Warm Up Roof
M   The Dark Heart
N   SE End of Comanche Canyon
O   Pigs in Space Buttress

P   The Great Wall
Q   The Doldrums
R   The Hidden Forest
S   Donkey Show Boulder

CHAPTER 2

EAST MOUNTAIN

Descriptions go counterclockwise around East Mountain, starting at the campground. If you aren't registered for the campground, you may not park there. Most of the East Mountain areas are easily approached from the East parking lot. The Donkey Show Boulder is most quickly approached by walking on the trail south from the campground through the pass between East Mountain and East Spur (Tabloid Pass).

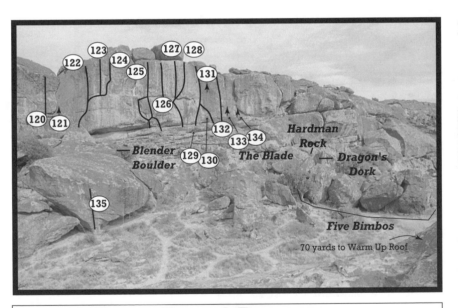

DRAGON'S WALL AND DRAGON'S DEN

120 Bob's Day Off 40 feet 5.11+
121 Short Dihedral 35 feet 5.9
122 Danger Bird 55 feet 5.11+ ★
123 Dangling Nerd 60 feet 5.11-TR ★
124 Ranger Turd 60 feet 5.11+TR
125 The Skidmark 60 feet 5.11+TR
126 Dragon's Breath 60 feet 5.12TR
127 Tlaloc Straight Up 60 feet 5.12 ★

128 Tlaloc 60 feet 5.12- TR ★★
129 A Dog's Life 60 feet 5.12 ★
130 Dog Legs And Feet 55 feet 5.10+ ★★
131 Save and Gain With Lobo 55 feet 5.6
132 Krispy Kritters 55 feet 5.11 TR
133 Dragon's Waltz 55 feet 5.8
134 Death and Texas 55 feet 5.10
135 Cactus Stupidity 28 feet 5.12 TR ★

BLENDER BOULDER

136   The Osterizer 15 feet V2 ★
137   Tri Hard 15 feet V4 ★

BLENDER BOULDER

138   The Ostracizer 16 feet V2 SD
139   Hobbit In A Blender 15 feet V4 ★★★

THE DRAGON'S DEN

The Dragon's Den boulders are located atop the major gully between the campground and the pass between East and North Mountains.

BLENDER BOULDER

This boulder is 10 yards east of Cactus Stupidity Rock.

136   **The Osterizer 15 feet V2** ★

137   **Tri Hard 15 feet V4** ★

138   **The Ostracizer 16 feet V2 SD**

139   **Hobbit In A Blender 15 feet V4** ★★★ Start low on two finger holds a foot apart and 5 feet above the dirt. Was V5 before some goober chiseled the starting hold.

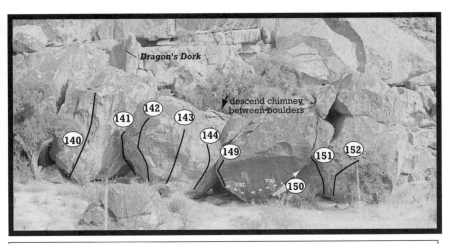

THE FIVE BIMBOS

140 *The Little Spermaid 20 feet V0*
141 *I Own It 15 feet V3 ★ (6 feet left of #142)*
142 *3 Star Arête 20 feet V2 ★★★ (V4 ★★ SD)*
143 *Texas Happy Hour 22 feet 5.13– TR ★*
144 *Red 22 feet V5*
149 *Assault Of The Killer Bimbos 10 feet V5 ★*
var. The New Map of Hell 20 feet V12 ★★
SD (off route big hold on #149)

150 *Kissing Cousins 20 feet V2 ★*
var. No Rebate 26 feet V5 ★ SD
151 *Cannibal Women In The Avocado Jungle Of*
Death 15 feet V6 ★ (V8 ★★ SD)
152 *Caged Heat 17 feet 5.12 TR ★*

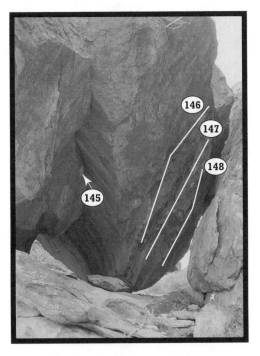

FIVE BIMBOS, SOUTH SIDE

145 *DG Crack 12 feet V2*
146 *NC17 17 feet V6 ★ BL*
147 *Babia Majora 15 feet V6 BL*
148 *Sorority Babes In The Slimeball Bowl-*
A-Rama 15 feet V3 ★

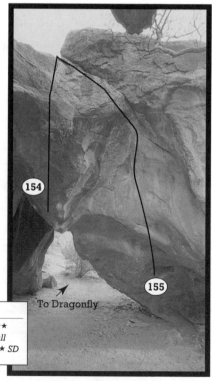

HARDMAN ROCK AREA

Hardman Rock is the rock immediately southeast of the Dragon's Dork. An oak tree grows between the two rocks. Access this well hidden boulder either by scrambling around the south side of the Dragon's Dork or drop in from the north along the east side of The Blade

HARDMAN ROCK

153 **Dragonfly (aka Dogmatics) 21 feet V5 ★★★** The left hand finish is a bit harder, but has a much safer landing. A hard sit down start has been added.

154 **Dry Dock 15 feet V7 ★★★** Either hug the bottom of the keel and fire up and right to a hueco, or do a huge swing from the ground to get started.

155 **Serves You Right (aka Full Service) 25 feet V10 ★★★ SD** The standup start from the low boulder is Lip Service (17 feet V4 ★).

> **HARDMAN ROCK**
> 153 Dragonfly (aka
>   Dogmatics) 21 feet V5
>   ★★★

> **HARDMAN ROCK**
> 154 Dry Dock 15 feet V7 ★★★
> 155 Serves You Right (aka Full
>   Service) 25 feet V10 ★★★ SD

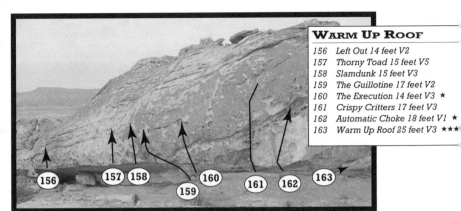

WARM UP ROOF

156	Left Out 14 feet V2
157	Thorny Toad 15 feet V5
158	Slamdunk 15 feet V3
159	The Guillotine 17 feet V2
160	The Execution 14 feet V3 ★
161	Crispy Critters 17 feet V3
162	Automatic Choke 18 feet V1 ★
163	Warm Up Roof 25 feet V3 ★★★

WARM UP ROOF

The Warm Up Roof lies atop the rocky slabs on the other side of the gully 70 yards west from the Dragon's Den (see the Dragon's Den photo). Its 140 foot long roof band faces west, away from the Dragon's Den. Situated between the Warm Up Roof and the Dragon's Den, and visible from much of the Dragon's Den, is the low, east-facing Kid's Stuff Wall. Descend to the south.

156 Left Out 14 feet V2 Start with hands at lip.

157 Thorny Toad 15 feet V5 Start in hueco 4 feet back from lip.

158 Slamdunk 15 feet V3 Leap to grab small holds at the lip (the crux), then finish straight up.

159 The Guillotine 17 feet V2

160 The Execution 14 feet V3 ★ Start at a first digit flake on the lip, or add a grade and start from the back of the roof.

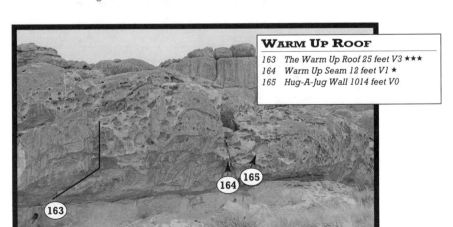

WARM UP ROOF

163	The Warm Up Roof 25 feet V3 ★★★
164	Warm Up Seam 12 feet V1 ★
165	Hug-A-Jug Wall 1014 feet V0

161 **Crispy Critters 17 feet V3** Start on the horizontal crack. Climb straight up the wall using a crispy sharp flake as the first hold after the starter crack.

162 **Automatic Choke 18 feet V1** ★ Start on the horizontal crack.

163 **The Warm Up Roof 25 feet V3** ★★★ Start on the horizontal crack at the back.

164 **Warm Up Seam 12 feet V1** ★

165 **Hug-A-Jug Wall 1014 feet V0**

SE end of Comanche Canyon

Dark Heart

Tanks For The Mammaries

COMANCHE CANYON (AS VIEWED FROM ATOP THE DAM)

COMANCHE CANYON (AKA MESCALERO CANYON)

Comanche Canyon is the major canyon on the north side of East Mountain. To get there, start at the East Parking Lot. Walk south through the gap where East and North Mountains come closest to each other then continue walking along the base of East Mountain until you run into a 20 foot tall stone dam. Comanche Canyon is the drainage blocked by this dam. The name is a misnomer, Comanches didn't live at Hueco Tanks. The rangers call this drainage Mescalero Canyon.

THE DARK HEART

The Dark Heart is at the extreme southeast end of Comanche Canyon, 30 yards uphill (northeast) of Water Dog Wall. A huge juniper guards the entrance. An even bigger boulder caps the Dark Heart Boulder complex. To approach the Dark Heart walk to the south end of Comanche Canyon, past Water Dog Wall on your right, to where Tanks for the Mammaries blocks the end of the canyon. Head up slabs between boulders northeast of Tanks for the Mammaries to reach the juniper and northeast of it the Dark Heart Boulders.

166 **Dark Heart Roof 18 feet V0+ ★★** Climb the line between the brown and tan rock to the roof formed by the huge caprock above. Reach behind you to holds under the roof. Undercling out then swing your feet across to the nearby rock to the southeast.

167 **Red Fox 12 feet V2**

168 **William's Lectric Shave 11 feet V4** The thin sharp face 5 feet right of the prow. Start off a small immobile rock at the base.

169 **Rocket Boosters 11 feet V2** Start immediately right of the immobile cheat stone of William's Lectric Shave.

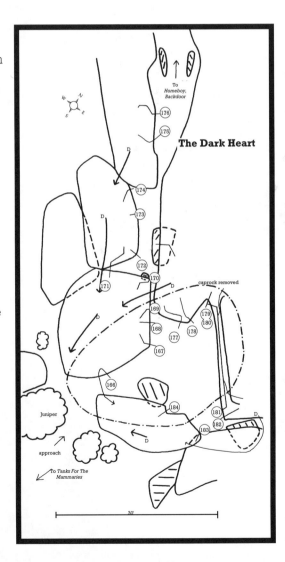

The Dark Heart

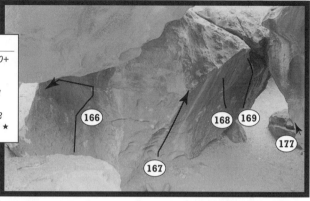

170   **Darth Vader 13 feet V1** Climb the arête between the north and east faces. Traverse a crack right to top out. The base boulder is off route.

171   **Something Different 15 feet V7 ★★★** Start off the good incut flakes 5 feet off the ground.

172   **The Bear 13 feet V4 ★**

173   **Politics Or Pontiacs 12 feet V4 ★**

174   **Spaceship Romex 12 feet V0+**

175   **Jiffy Pop 20 feet V4 ★** Via the fingertip seam.

176   **Swirl Wall 18 feet V3** Start anywhere 6-10 feet left of the detached flake under the right end of the wall. Tops out at the right side of the swirling rock. Freaky moves, some friable holds.

177   **The Ventral Fin
      15 feet V1 ★**

178   **Cowboyectomy 17 feet V3★ scary** Holds on the Ventral. Fin are off route for the hands.

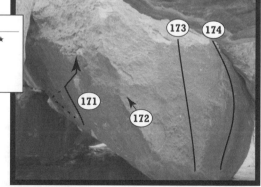

179 **Dark Angel 19 feet V0** ★★

180 **Heartbreak Traverse (left to right, high) 30 feet V0+**
Finish at roof level around the right corner of the sizable caprock.

181 **Heartbreak Traverse (right to left, low) 30 feet V3** ★
scary Start up Moonwalk, but move to the left of the huecos once your feet are 6 feet up. Continue straight left around the arête to a 2 foot long shelf angling down and left. Crank or throw from the shelf for the 5 foot long angling ledge to your left. Hand traverse this to it's left end then up to the roof and top out left.

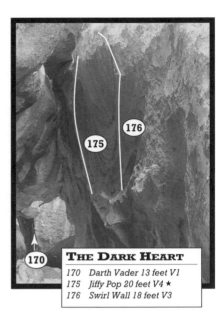

THE DARK HEART

170 *Darth Vader 13 feet V1*
175 *Jiffy Pop 20 feet V4* ★
176 *Swirl Wall 18 feet V3*

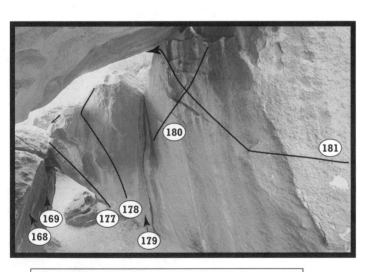

THE DARK HEART

168 *Red Fox 12 feet V2*
169 *William's Lectric Shave 11 feet V4*
177 *The Ventral Fin 15 feet V1* ★
178 *Cowboyectomy 17 feet V3* ★
179 *Dark Angel 19 feet V0* ★★
180 *Heartbreak Traverse (left to right, high) 30 feet V0+*
181 *Heartbreak Traverse (right to left, low) 30 feet V3* ★

182   **Moonwalk 21 feet V0**
★

183   **Botch-A-Notch 16 feet V1**   Start in the inverted notch between boulders. Finish in the notch above. Use both rocks. Lousy. A better variant doesn't use the left wall. Start in the inverted notch and head out right onto the face and up the wall avoiding the left arête above the notch (V5 BL scary).

184   **The Pipeloader 14 feet V2**   The 3 foot tall boulder at your right is off route.

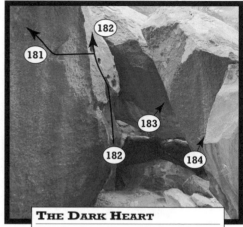

THE DARK HEART

181   *Heartbreak Traverse (right to left, low) 30 feet V3* ★
182   *Moonwalk 21 feet V0* ★
183   *Botch-A-Notch 16 feet V1*
184   *The Pipeloader 14 feet V2*

SOUTHEAST END OF COMMANCHE CANYON

185   **Tanks For the Mammaries 35 feet 5.13–** ★★   This is the severely overhanging hueco wall at the south end of Comanche Canyon.

186   **Boys' Town 35 feet 5.13+**   Bring big gear for the huecos between the bolts.

187   **Murray Toprope 20 feet 5.12 TR**

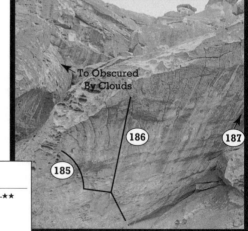

To Obscured By Clouds

SOUTHEAST END OF COMMANCHE CANYON

185   *Tanks For the Mammaries 35 feet 5.13–*★★
186   *Boys' Town 35 feet 5.13+*
187   *Murray Toprope 20 feet 5.12 TR*

PIGS IN SPACE BUTTRESS

Pigs In Space Buttress is the 150 foot buttress on the northwest side of the entrance to Comanche Canyon. Comanche Canyon Dam is 140 yards left (southeast) of Pigs In Space Buttress. To descend, walk north down the sloped rock then turn left towards a ledge with a tree to the east. Climb down the hueco covered wall east of the tree to the base of Plastic Fantastic.
NOTE: BEWARE OF THE BEES THAT RESIDE BETWEEN PORK SHUTTLE AND PIGS IN SPACE 10 FEET RIGHT OF THE GREAT WHITE HUECO. THEY HAVE ATTACKED MANY CLIMBERS.

188   **Plastic Fantastic 40 feet 5.11 TR ★★★** Top rope ever steepening rock 5 to 10 feet left of the black streak. Follow the huecos to a small notch in the lip of the overhang. Access the anchors by scrambling around the corner to the left (5.6).

   Variation: Plastic Surgery 40 feet 5.11+ TR★★ Finish up the right-facing flake/crack halfway between the Plastic Fantastic notch to the left and the black streak notch to the right.

189   **Death Dihedral 120 feet 5.8 ★**

190   **Pork Shuttle 140 feet 5.10 ★★** BEWARE OF BEES Climb the first part of Death Dihedral to the alcove 35 feet up. Continue up the right-hand wall of the corner on huecos to a short, right-slanting crack below The Great White Hueco. The Great White Hueco is 6 feet right of Death Dihedral's tree. Traverse left to a hueco with a

PIGS IN SPACE BUTTRESS

188   Plastic Fantastic 40 feet 5.11 TR ★★★
189   Death Dihedral 120 feet 5.8 ★
190   Pork Shuttle 140 feet 5.10 ★★
191   Pigs In Space 140 feet 5.10 ★★
192   Pig Riders 150 feet 5.10 ★

bolt inside, then climb straight up and right, following good huecos to a bolt and the steep face above.

var. Pigs To Pork 140 feet 5.10+ ★★★ BEWARE OF BEES Start on Pigs In Space and go directly up and left to The Great White Hueco, bypassing the belay ledge. Finish up Pork Shuffle. This route is done in one long pitch and requires many slings to reduce rope drag.

191 Pigs In Space 140 feet 5.10 ★★ BEWARE OF BEES Begin in the chimney with a chockstone at head level (base of Death Dihedral). Step up right from the chockstone to the base of the overhanging rock. Follow good huecos and 2 bolts in a brown water streak to a stance left of a ledge. Step right to the ledge and belay. The second pitch climbs straight up to easier ground.

192 Pig Riders 150 feet 5.10 ★ Start on a ramp (20 feet right of Death Dihedral's base) which leads to a bulge 30 feet up. Climb the bulge on its right side (1 bolt) and continue on steep rock past 2 pins to a headwall with a bolt at its base. Traverse left under the headwall, to a prow and climb straight up.

193 Pigs On A Rope 35 feet 5.10-5.11 TR

194 Kings Highway 150 feet 5.9★

THE GREAT WALL

This is the large, overhanging wall which dominates the northwest side of East Mountain.

195 Star Dust 70 feet 5.12 ★★★ This line is 30 feet right of a right-facing corner with a honeycomb halfway up. Scramble up to the large ledge with the tree. Rope up and follow the protection. A wired nut placement is useful and often fixed. 4 bolts, 2 bolt anchor.

196 Tarts of Horsham 75 feet 5.12+ ★★ Start at the right end of the ledge, 60 feet right of the honeycomb corner. Angle right past two bolts. At the third bolt go straight up to the top.

197 Wasp Warrior 130 feet 5.11 ★ 60 feet to the right of Tarts of Horsham is an energetic problem made all the more exciting by the numerous wasp nests in this area. There are two ways to mount the ledge at the start of this climb: start with a direct bolt protected boulder problem-type move, or traverse in from the right where the ledge is closest to the ground level. The line then departs from the highest point of the ledge. Ascend straight toward and over the small overhanging bulge halfway up (4 more bolts). Continue to the top of the wall for the belay. Medium sized nuts are useful.

THE GREAT WALL

192 Pig Riders 150 feet 5.10 ★	195 Star Dust 70 feet 5.12 ★★★
193 Pigs On A Rope 35 feet 5.10-5.11 TR	196 Tarts of Horsham 75 feet 5.12+ ★★
194 Kings Highway 150 feet 5.9 ★	197 Wasp Warrior 130 feet 5.11 ★

SOUTHWEST SIDE OF EAST MOUNTAIN

This area is embodies four parallel, east to west trending "canyons": The Trade Winds, The Doldrums, The Hidden Forest, and The Watchtower. The routes in the canyons are on the northwest faces. The four canyons that make up this general area can be seen from the north end of the Main Dam.

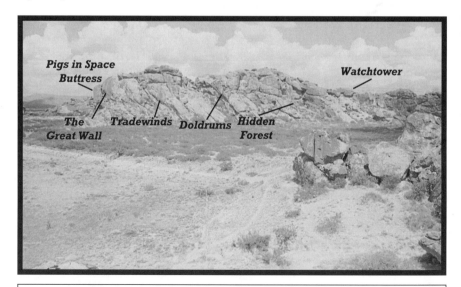

SOUTHWEST SIDE OF EAST MOUNTAIN

**THE
DOLDRUMS**

198   *The Wild, Wild,
        West 120 feet
        5.12–★*
199   *Central Latitudes 70
        feet 5.11+ ★★★*
200   *Horses Latitudes 50
        feet 5.11 ★★★*

THE DOLDRUMS

*This canyon features the biggest wall on the southwest side of East Mountain.
Three routes start 100 yards up the canyon on a big ledge which is accessed
from the right. Rappel from atop Horse Latitudes or scramble off to the west.*

   198   **The Wild, Wild, West 120 feet 5.12–** ★ A convenient belay ledge
           is located 5 feet from the top. Bring many slings to prevent rope
           drag.

   199   **Central Latitudes 70 feet 5.11+** ★★★ Step left from the large
           sloping ledge to the left-facing dihedral as for Wild, Wild, West.
           Climb up and right on spectacular grey overhanging rock past three
           bolts. When the angle eases move right to the tree above Horse
           Latitudes or continue (5.11) on clean gear straight up to the top.

   200   **Horses Latitudes 50 feet 5.11** ★★★ The obvious overhanging
           hand crack. Tape is recommended.

HIDDEN FOREST

*This canyon is easily identified by its steep, brown northwest face and the
huge roc block which caps the back of the canyon. Most people climb the
routes fro. visible Sun to Lizard King only to the horizontal break 60 feet up
where anchors can be set. To descend from the horizontal break traverse left
to a 5.5 downclimb at the left end of the wall, below the big roof block.*

   201   **Invisible Sun 55 feet 5.10+** ★ Climb over the small roof on the left
           side of the wall above the 5 foot long horizontal Friend slot. This is
           15 feet left of Waiting For The Sun.

HIDDEN FOREST

201 *Invisible Sun 55 feet 5.10+* ★	205 *Now It's Dark 100 feet 5.12–*
202 *Waiting For The Sun 55 feet 5.11* ★★	206 *My Captain 60 feet 5.11* ★
203 *Gecko Master 60 feet 5.11* ★★	207 *Captain Reality 90 feet 5.10* ★
204 *Lizard King 65 feet 5.11* ★★	

202 **Waiting For The Sun 55 feet 5.11** ★★ This route climbs a steep hueco line 18 feet left of Gecko Master. 1 pin, 1 bolt.

203 **Gecko Master 60 feet 5.11** ★★ This route follows the orange water streak up the center of the wall past one pin and one bolt.

204 **Lizard King 65 feet 5.11** ★★ Climb the first 40 feet of Gecko Master to the pin. Traverse right on the horizontal crack 2 feet below the pin for 10 feet, then climb straight up huecos past one bolt to the horizontal break.

205 **Now It's Dark 100 feet 5.12–** This is the white streak 25 feet right of Lizard King. Start from the first big chockstone uphill (left) from My Captain.

206 **My Captain 60 feet 5.11** ★

207 **Captain Reality 90 feet 5.10** ★ Traverse the obvious severely left-leaning crack for 50 feet to a bulge, then climb straight up a steep line of flakes past two bolts to a two bolt belay on a ledge 60 feet up.

THE DONKEY SHOW BOULDER

*The Donkey Show Boulder is located at ground level along the south flank of
East Mountain 110 yards west of the Tabloid boulders (the pass between East
Mountain and East Spur). The southwest face of the Donkey Show Boulder,
with it's concentration of hard bouldering and UV rays, is a popular hang on
cold winter days.*

208   **Nuns And Donkeys 15 feet V6** ★   Start in an undercling 4 feet
      right of the left end of the southwest face. Climb straight up the
      sharp flakes above. Starting on holds above the undercling knocks
      off a V grade.

209   **Left Donkey Show 16 feet V5** ★★★   Start on a blunt horn, 6 feet up
      the left side of the 3 foot wide black stain. Work into a fingertip
      undercling at the top of the stain. Head left to the horizontal jam slot
      then up and slightly left to the top.

210   **Buttcracker (aka Right Donkey Show) 16 feet V5** ★★★ **BL**   Climb
      straight up the 3 foot wide tan streak with the white boarders.

211   **El Burro 13 feet V3** ★★   Harder than it looks. A sit down start adds
      length to this, but not difficulty.

212   **Beast Of Burden 13 feet V4** ★   Done with a sit down start, this
      problem becomes harder, but not a full grade.

213   **Steel Toed Gourd Kickers 13 feet V3**

214   **Two Moves For Sister Sarah 12 feet V3**

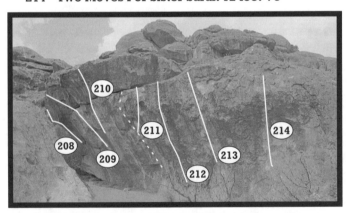

THE DONKEY SHOW BOULDER

208   *Nuns And Donkeys 15 feet V6* ★
209   *Left Donkey Show 16 feet V5* ★★★
210   *Buttcracker (aka Right Donkey Show) 16 feet V5* ★★★ *BL*
211   *El Burro 13 feet V3* ★★
212   *Beast Of Burden 13 feet V4* ★
213   *Steel Toed Gourd Kickers 13 feet V3*
214   *Two Moves For Sister Sarah 12 feet V3*

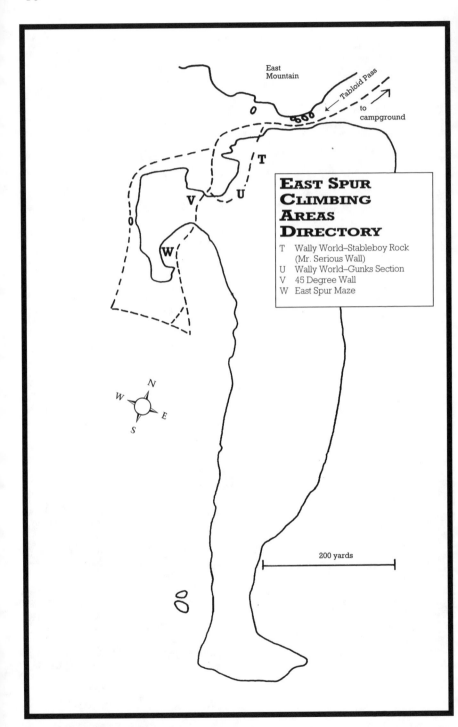

EAST SPUR CLIMBING AREAS DIRECTORY

T   Wally World–Stableboy Rock
    (Mr. Serious Wall)
U   Wally World–Gunks Section
V   45 Degree Wall
W   East Spur Maze

200 yards

CHAPTER 3

EAST SPUR

Descriptions for the East Spur go counterclockwise around the mountain, starting at the north end just west of Tabloid Pass (the pass between East Mountain and East Spur). The quickest approach is along the trail exiting the south end of the campground. Don't park in the campground if you aren't registered there.

WALLY WORLD

Wally World is used to refer to the boulders above the 45 Degree Wall, 50-100 yards to the east. It's broken into 2 sections in this book – the Stableboy Rock area to the north and east of 45 Degree Wall, and the Gunks Area to the southeast of 45 Degree Wall.

NORTH END OF EAST SPUR

STABLEBOY ROCK AREA (MR. SERIOUS WALL)

Stableboy Rock (Mr. Serious Wall) lies a few yards away from the main cliff which overhangs Stableboy Rock's east face. It can be found by walking southwest along the base of the main cliff starting at Tabloid Pass. After 115 yards, do not drop elevation from the pass) you should see Indian paintings under the overhang to your left (east) and a juniper in front of you. Stableboy Rock is the enormous boulder 20 yards south of the juniper. A tunnel squeezes along the base of it's east face. To descend downclimb the north side of the northwest arete.

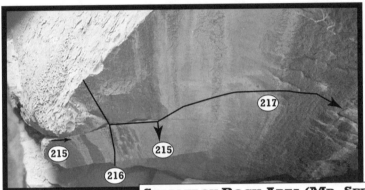

STABLEBOY ROCK AREA (MR. SERIOUS WALL LEFT)

215 Little Debbies 22 feet V0+
216 Mr. Smiley 17 feet V9 ★★★BL
217 Get Serious (aka Mr. Serious Wall Traverse) 55 feet V11 ★★★ BL

STABLEBOY ROCK AREA (MR. SERIOUS WALL RIGHT)

217 Get Serious (aka Mr. Serious Wall Traverse) 55 feet V11★★★ BL
218 Mr. Serious 14 feet V8 ★★★ a-b-c
219 Dead Legends 13 feet V5 ★★ a-d-f
220 A Good Day For Swiss Crisp Mix 16 feet V10 ★★★ e-d-b-c
Other Variatons:
Dead Serious 18 feet V10 ★★★ SD e-d-a-b-c
Serious Legends 25 feet V9 ★★ f-d-a-b-c

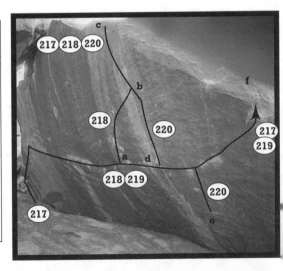

215 Little Debbies 22 feet V0+ Hand traverse the flake at the left end of the east face. Start at the left end of the flake. At the right end, step off to the boulder behind.

216 Mr. Smiley 17 feet V9 ★★★ BL Start on the horizontal crack under the roof.

217 Get Serious (aka Mr. Serious Wall Traverse) 55 feet V11 ★★★ BL This climbed Mr. Smiley up to the Little Debbies crack, traversed the wall right to Mr. Serious, then finished up that.

218 Mr. Serious 14 feet V8 ★★★ Do a-b-c The small holds right of the cream colored streak are on route.

219 Dead Legends 13 feet V5 ★★ Do a-d-f.

220 A Good Day For Swiss Crisp Mix 16 feet V10 ★ ★★ low SD Do e-d-b-c.

Other Variations:

Dead Serious 18 feet V10 ★★★ SD Do e-d-a-b-c.

Serious Legends 25 feet V9 ★★ Do f-d-a-b-c Start with foot hooked at Dead Legends' lip.

WALLY WORLD — GUNKS SECTION

The Gunks section of Wally World is located 50 yards east of the 45 Degree Wall, atop slabs 40 to 50 feet above ground level.

GUNKS BOULDER

Jump off the east end to descend.

221 Fight Or Flight 16 feet V4 ★★★ Scary. The first hold is a left-facing flake with a cornish game hen size hueco behind it. It's 7 feet up on the right side of a whitish stained patch. V6 ★★★ with the sitdown start.

222 Straight Outta Conway 16 feet V5 ★ BL scary loose Start on the same first hold as Fight Or Flight.

GUNKS BOULDER

221 Fight Or Flight 16 feet V4 ★★★
222 Straight Outta Conway 16 feet V5 ★ BL
227 Y Chihuahua 13 feet V5 ★

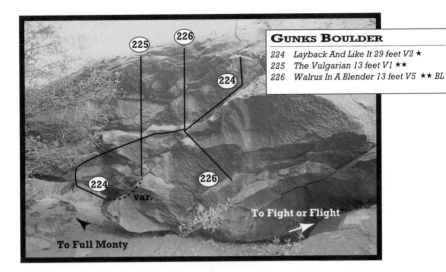

GUNKS BOULDER

224	*Layback And Like It 29 feet V2* ★
225	*The Vulgarian 13 feet V1* ★★
226	*Walrus In A Blender 13 feet V5* ★★ BL

To Fight or Flight

To Full Monty

223 **Full Monty 11 feet V11** ★★ Start on the same first hold as Layback And Like It. Climb up the south face.

224 **Layback And Like It 29 feet V2** ★ Crouch under the left side of the face, almost around the corner, to start on the left end of the sloping block next to the sotol. Either prostrate yourself across this sloping block to the right, or reach out the roof to a traverse flake. Traverse the wall right until the horizontal line takes you around the lip's right end.

225 **The Vulgarian 13 feet V1**★★ Start low for added challenge.

226 **Walrus In A Blender 13 feet V5** ★★ SD Either move left to top out as for The Vulgarian, or do a tougher top out straight up.

227 **Y Chihuahua 13 feet V5** ★ Start low, with a fingerlock right next to where the rocks touch.

BAD RELIGION WALL

This west-facing wall is 10 yards northeast of the Gunks Boulder.

228 **All The Idiots 15 feet V3** Begin on huecos 4 feet up and 5 feet right of the face's left end. Use the prow on the left to top out.

Variation: (21 feet V5) Start at beginning of New Religion, then traverse left into All The Idiots.

229 **New Religion 16 feet V7** ★★★ Start on a right facing flake 4½ feet up.

Variation: Brand New Religion V8. Does the crux of New Religion, then traverses right along and just beneath the lip. Bad landing for a move or two.

THE 45 DEGREE WALL

The 45 Degree Wall is at the back (south end) of a cul-de-sac in the north end of East Spur. It is at ground level and will be found 100 yards south of That's My Daughter. The best way to find it is to start at Tabloid Pass (the pass between East Mountain and East Spur) and walk 75 yards west, dropping about 30 feet elevation from the pass, until you reach a 5-foot wide trail. Follow this wide trail another 75 yards to That's My Daughter where the trail forks. Take the left fork, heading south into the cul-de-sac. The trail initially points towards the 45 degree wall 80 yards to the south. A big juniper is on the wall's left.

BAD RELIGION WALL

228 *All The Idiots 15 feet V3*
229 *New Religion 16 feet V7* ★★★

230 **Melting Point 10 feet V0+** Start 27 feet left of the start of 45 degree Wall, just left of a rocky lump on the slab below. 2 vertical seams mark the line. Crank from the flake to a point at the lip and waddle over.

231 **Frigid 12 feet V1** Turn the lip 10 feet left of Boiling Point. Start between the rocky lumps on the slab.

232 **Icy Hot 11 feet V2 BL** Mantel the lip 5 feet left of Boiling Point.

THE 45 DEGREE WALL

230 *Melting Point 10 feet V0+*
231 *Frigid 12 feet V1*
232 *Icy Hot 11 feet V2 BL*
233 *Boiling Point (AKA The Texas Mantel) 13 feet V3*
234 *Double Boiler 20 feet V7 ★★★ SD*
235 *The 45 Degree Wall 24 feet V5 ★★★★ SD*

233 **Boiling Point (AKA The Texas Mantel) 13 feet V3** Start 10 feet left of the start of 45 Degree Wall, at a flexing flake 7 feet above an 18 inch deep grinding hole. Please leave the hole empty and uncovered.

234 **Double Boiler 20 feet V7 ★★★ SD** Start at the base of the 45° Wall problem, then angle left ot finish up Boiling Point.

235 **The 45 Degree Wall 24 feet V5 ★★★★ SD** One of the coldest spots in the park, and one of the coolest. Bad landing if you fall off the lip moves. The grinding holes have been repeatedly filled up with dirt (and sometimes tapewads, butts, etc.) to smooth out the landing. Park officials do not considered this an acceptable use of the resource. Please leave these holes empty, as well as the one under Double Boiler and all others in the park.

236 **Absolute Zero 14 feet V3 BL scary** At the right end of the wall, 11 yards from 45 Degree Wall's start, is a thin walled football width hueco 8 feet up. Undercling this, hoping it doesn't snap, and keep chugging to the lip.

237 **The Deep Freeze 24 feet V1★ SD** The 45 degree Wall is actually a 3 foot thick zig zag flake at it's right end. Start sitting down and hand traverse out to the lip.

EAST SPUR MAZE

South of The 45 Degree Wall is another cul-de-sac in the rocks, this one opening to the south. The East Spur Maze is the group of boulders on the southwest side of this cul-de-sac. Sheltered from the wind, it is one of the warmest areas in the park. Walking over the pass atop the 45 Degree Wall is the quickest approach.

GODZILLATRON BOULDER

This 25 foot tall boulder is the furthest boulder south of this size in the East Spur Maze. To descend, jump off the south end onto a smaller boulder.

238 **Thumpasaurus 25 feet V0+ scary** Climb the east face topping out in the notch on the left end of the

EAST SPUR MAZE SEEN FROM THE PASS ABOVE 45 DEGREE WALL

summit. The crux is near the top.

239 **Jingus Bells 23 feet V5 ★★★ BL** An even scarier variation starts up Jingus Bells then moves left to finish up the arete to its left.

240 **Slayride 20 feet V2 ★ BL**

241 **Funkicidal Vibrations 17 feet V2 BL** scary loose

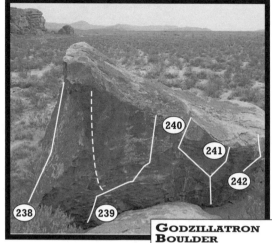

242 **The Godzillatron Cush 14 feet V3 ★** Start with a jump to a 2 hand jug 8½ feet up.

GODZILLATRON BOULDER

238 Thumpasaurus 25 feet V0+
239 Jingus Bells 23 feet V5 ★★★ BL
240 Slayride 20 feet V2 ★ BL
241 Funkicidal Vibrations 17 feet V2 BL
242 The Godzillatron Cush 14 feet V3 ★

WHEATIES WALL

This is the boulder found between Godzillatron and Toejam boulders, but not seen on the photo on the previous page. Descend to the northeast.

243 **Torch Song 38 feet V5 ★★ SD** Traverse right across the wall without using the lip.

244 **Garvey's Ghost 9 feet V0 ★**

245 **Burning Spear 12 feet V0+ ★** Tack on a grade for a sit down start.

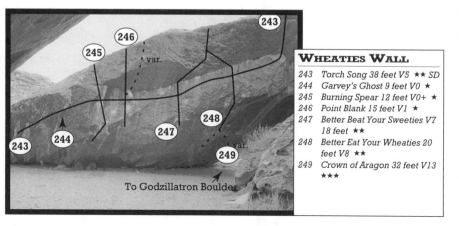

WHEATIES WALL

243 Torch Song 38 feet V5 ★★ SD
244 Garvey's Ghost 9 feet V0 ★
245 Burning Spear 12 feet V0+ ★
246 Point Blank 15 feet V1 ★
247 Better Beat Your Sweeties V7 18 feet ★★
248 Better Eat Your Wheaties 20 feet V8 ★★
249 Crown of Aragon 32 feet V13 ★★★

To Godzillatron Boulder

246 **Point Blank 15 feet V1** ★ From a sit down start this is V3★

Variation: Point Blunk 16 feet V4 Move right from the flake to a two fingertip pocket at the overhang's lip. Crank off this pocket to the top.

247 **Better Beat Your Sweeties V7 18 feet** ★★

248 **Better Eat Your Wheaties 20 feet V8**★★ Start 6 feet right of Better Beat Your Sweeties with your left fingers behind a thin incut flake 6 feet up, and the right hand on a flake just above the right side of a grey patch 5 feet up. V9 from a sit down start.

249 **Crown of Aragorn 32 feet V13** ★★★ Starts at the far right end of the wall and traverses 12 feet left to finish up Better Eat Your Wheaties.

TEN FOOT WALL

250 **Black And Blue 12 feet V1** ★★ Start sitting or standing.

251 **Gangbanging That Wide Crack 13 feet V3**

252 **The Cowpuncher 13 feet V4** ★ Start on the 2 foot tall bad landing boulder. Pinch tinies to slap the rough sloper above. Big holds follow.

SLIM PICKINS FACE

Slim Pickins Face is the north-facing wall 12 feet around the corner right of Black And Blue. It contains one of the few hard slab problems at Hueco Tanks.

253 **Fats Domino 13 feet V0 or 20 feet V0+** ★★ **BL** A 20 foot variation goes up a move, then finger traverses the right angling seam line, topping out at the green lichen.

254 **Chubby Checker 16 feet V0+** ★

255 **Slim Pickins 17 feet V5** ★★ Bad landing if hit wrong.

256 **Slim Whitman 22 feet V1** ★ **scary** Start on the ground. High crux.

257 **Saab Story 24 feet V1 BL scary** The following contrived problem is where the northern descent from Slim Pickins hops down from the lip of an overhung off-width.

DIHEDRAL ROCK

258 **The Jigsaw Puzzle 16 feet V5** ★★ **BL**

Variation 1: starting at the left end of the traverse reduces it to V3.

Variation 2: going straight up (scary and loose) is V6.

259 **Sex With Oprah 11 feet V2** Start just right of a foot tall slab at the left (west) end of the south face.

260 **The Sizzler 12 feet V4** Turn the lip 3 feet left of Horny.

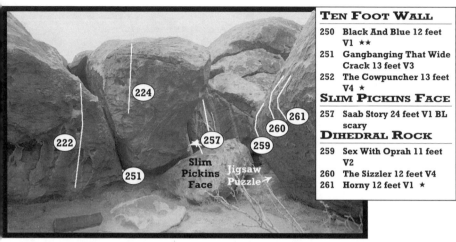

TEN FOOT WALL

250 **Black And Blue 12 feet V1** ★★

251 **Gangbanging That Wide Crack 13 feet V3**

252 **The Cowpuncher 13 feet V4** ★

SLIM PICKINS FACE

257 **Saab Story 24 feet V1 BL scary**

DIHEDRAL ROCK

259 **Sex With Oprah 11 feet V2**

260 **The Sizzler 12 feet V4**

261 **Horny 12 feet V1** ★

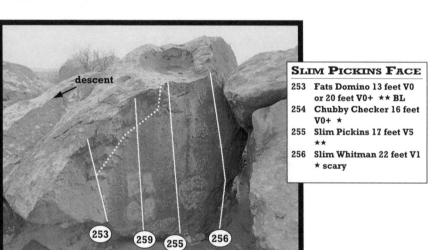

SLIM PICKINS FACE

253 **Fats Domino 13 feet V0 or 20 feet V0+** ★★ **BL**

254 **Chubby Checker 16 feet V0+** ★

255 **Slim Pickins 17 feet V5** ★★

256 **Slim Whitman 22 feet V1** ★ **scary**

261 **Horny 12 feet V1** ★ Surmount the highest point on the lip of the south face overhang. At this point, the lip is graced with several rounded horns.

262 **Bildo 11 feet V0**

263 **The Flexin' Texan 12 feet V0+**

264 **The Globetrotter 10 feet V0+**

265 **Strip Show Faux Pas 10 feet V0+**

266 **The Lactator 9 feet V0** ★

267 **The Dicktator 12 feet V0+ SD**

268 The French Fry 10 feet V0+ SD

269 Italy Overthrown 9 feet V2 Start with fingers on a flake 5 feet up. This flake looks like an upside-down map of Italy.

270 **This Is Your Brain On Drugs 10 feet V2 ★ SD** Start on flakes 4½ feet up.

271 **Bilbo Gets Buggered 7 feet V2 ★ SD**

DIHEDRAL ROCK

258   The Jigsaw Puzzle 16 feet V5 ★★ BL

descent

THE BOMB BOULDER

272 **The Javelina 25 feet V8 ★** Left to right traverse. Step off or top out.

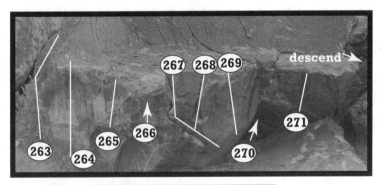

descend

DIHEDRAL ROCK

263   The Flexin' Texan 12 feet V0+
264   The Globetrotter 10 feet V0+
265   Strip Show Faux Pas 10 feet V0+
266   The Lactator 9 feet V0 ★
267   The Dicktator 12 feet V0+ SD
268   The French Fry 10 feet V0+ SD
269   Italy Overthrown 9 feet V2
270   This Is Your Brain On Drugs 10 feet V2 ★ SD
271   Bilbo Gets Buggered 7 feet V2 ★ SD

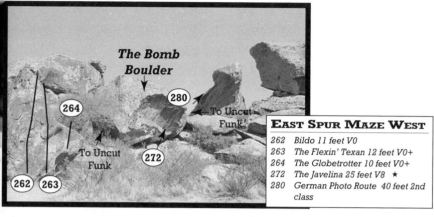

The Bomb Boulder

UNCUT FUNK AREA (AKA THE OFFICE)

The following boulder problems are in the corridor on the southwest side of The Bomb boulder. Enter the corridor at the south end of The Bomb boulder. Uncut Funk is at the dead end at the northwest end of the corridor. Uncut Funk can also be reached by scrambling around the northwest end of The Bomb Boulder, but is harder to find this way.

273   **Nobody 10 feet V6** ★ Low start in sloping scoop.

    Variation: Funky Ring-Eye V9 starts sitting down beneath Uncut Funk, moves left to the scoop, and finishes up Nobody.

274   **Nobody's Funky 15 feet V7** ★ Start as for Nobody, finish up the top of Uncut Funk.

275   **Nobody's Ugly After Two AM 13 feet V10** ★ Start on Nobody, climb to the lip of Uncut Funk, downclimb the crux bulge of Uncut Funk, then traverse right to finish up a 4-inch wide left-facing corner.

276   **Uncut Funk 13 feet V7** ★★ Start with both hands underclinging the melon. From the sit down start this is V8.

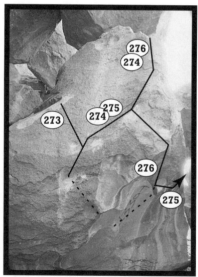

GERMAN PHOTO ROUTE BOULDER

The following problems are in the dark corridor underneath the southeast end of the German Photo Route boulder.

277   The Dark Flower length and grade variable★ The overhanging handcrack is V0+ if started high (in the handjams), or as hard as you want it to be if you start further and further back in the offwidth sit down start.

278   Nicole Route 15 feet V11 ★★ SD

279   Glas Roof 15 feet V9 ★★ SD This climb will go without the doctored pocket at the lip (the moves have been done, but not linked from the start).

280   German Photo Route (aka Klingon Warship) 40 feet 2nd class This climbs the 40 foot tongue of rock thrusting eastward over the low boulders 20 yards north of the East Spur Maze. Walk up the tongue to the lip, taking care not to trip over two bolts on the way (empty sleeves at presstime).

Variation: (5.11) Instead of walking to the top, hand traverse rotting flakes across the southern edge of the tongue.

GERMAN PHOTO RTE BOULDER

277   *The Dark Flower length and grade variable*
278   *Nicole Route 15 feet V11★★ SD*
279   *Glas Roof 15 feet V9 ★★ SD*

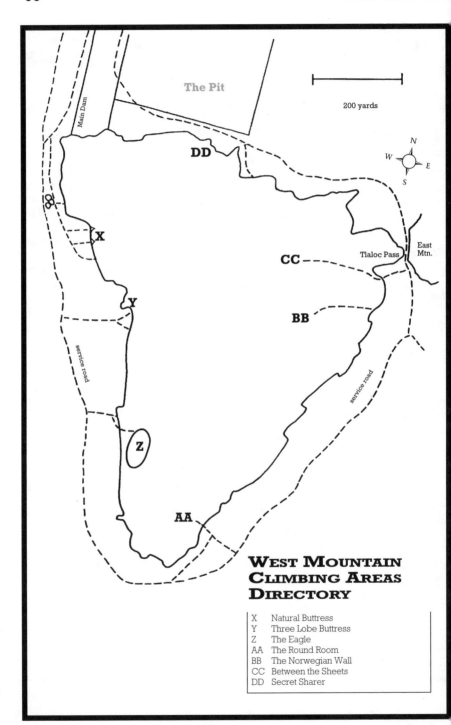

The Pit

200 yards

DD

N
W — E
S

East
Mtn.

Tlaloc Pass

CC

X

BB

Y

service road

service road

Z

AA

WEST MOUNTAIN CLIMBING AREAS DIRECTORY

X	Natural Buttress
Y	Three Lobe Buttress
Z	The Eagle
AA	The Round Room
BB	The Norwegian Wall
CC	Between the Sheets
DD	Secret Sharer

Main Dam

CHAPTER 4

WEST MOUNTAIN

Descriptions for West Mountain go counterclockwise around the mountain starting at the southwest end of the Main Dam.

NATURAL BUTTRESS

Walk 350 yards south from the Main Dam, along the western flank of West Mountain, to a steep north-facing wall. The Natural Buttress is flanked to the north by a shallow canyon with a big roof block capping the rear of the canyon. The descent off the top is tricky and hard to find. Walk east off the top, then turn south and scramble down the first canyon south of Natural Buttress.

281   **All Natural 35 feet 5.8**

282   **Supernatural Anesthetist 150 feet 5.12 ★★** Belay in the wide spot 20 feet over the roof. The second pitch climbs up the thin crack to a leftfacing dihedral, (5.10).

   Variation: Climb up buckets up and right after the roof.

283   **Mr. Natural 75 feet 5.11 ★** Four bolts; at presstime, the first two were hangerless, as were the belay bolts on top.

3 Lobe Buttress

Natural Buttress

Eagle

Main Dam

NATURAL BUTTRESS

281 *All Natural 35 feet 5.8*
282 *Supernatural Anesthetist 150 feet*
     5.12 ★★
283 *Mr. Natural 75 feet 5.11* ★

NATURAL BUTTRESS

284 *Iron Man 130 feet 5.10*
285 *Sunny Side Up 60 feet 5.12* ★
286 *Max Headroom 110 feet 5.11*
287 *Ramp to Hell 150 feet 5.10*

284 **Iron Man 130 feet 5.10**

285 **Sunny Side Up 60 feet 5.12** ★ Five bolts, two bolt anchor.

286 **Max Headroom 110 feet 5.11** Climb the first 40 feet of Ramp To
     Hell, stopping 15 feet above a console TV size block wedged
     against the ramp. Follow huecos and six bolts straight to the top
     and a two bolt anchor.

287 **Ramp to Hell 150 feet 5.10**

THREE-LOBE BUTTRESS

100 yards south of Natural Buttress is a wide boulder-strewn gully leading
up to a low point in the crest of West Mountain. 30 yards right (south) of this
low point is a three-lobed buttress. The right hand (southern) lobe has a
115-degree south face with the following two routes.

288 Natural Mystic 85 feet 5.11 ★

289 Huecool 80 feet 5.12 TR ★★★
5 bolts + 2 at anchor. The first
clip is well protected if you
place your own gear.

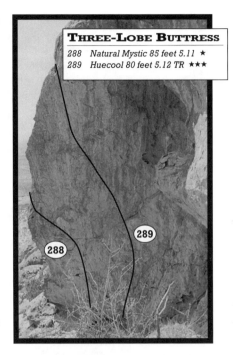

THREE-LOBE BUTTRESS

288 Natural Mystic 85 feet 5.11 ★
289 Huecool 80 feet 5.12 TR ★★★

THE EAGLE

*To descend The Eagle scramble down
easy rock on the east side.*

290 **The Gunfighter 100 feet
5.13– ★★**

Variation: After pulling the
bulge, follow the right leaning
crack 20 feet then belay. For
the second pitch, exit the
right- leaning crack on its left
and follow a striking 5.11+
thin crack straight up the
northeast face to the top of the
Eagle.

291 **When Legends Die 75 feet
5.13 ★★★** Seven bolts,
two-bolt anchor. Runout at
the top.

292 **Road To Nowhere 45
feet 5.11+ ★★** Climb the
steep rock on the corner
until the crack is reached.
Climb the severely
overhanging crack until it
ends, then lower off the
anchors.

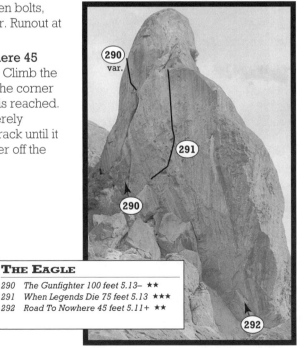

THE EAGLE

290 *The Gunfighter 100 feet 5.13– ★★*
291 *When Legends Die 75 feet 5.13 ★★★*
292 *Road To Nowhere 45 feet 5.11+ ★★*

The Round Room

THE ROUND ROOM

This is one of the more difficult to find bouldering spots in Hueco Tanks. Two possible approaches are given. Walk to the far south end of West Mountain (the end closest to Pete's). From the southernmost end of West Mountain's southernmost boulder walk 165 yards northeast along the wide dirt trail on West Mountain's southeast side. Turn left and walk 25 yards to meet the rocks. At this point a large oak tree grows in a corner in the rocks. The corner faces north, so you won't see it until you're even with it. Even then it's indistinct. 15 feet left of this oak is a small ailing oak at the toe of a 24 foot tall buttress (marked "Marcy, Pete" 5 feet above the base). If you've found yourself now, simply scramble up the vine covered slab to your west, (just right of the big healthy oak), past one 3rd class move, until you're in the Round Room (you'll gain 25 feet elevation). If you haven't found the approach slab yet try finding the 30 foot tall, 3 foot wide black water streak to it's right. This streak disappears into a group of trees at it's base. 28 yards left of the streak is the toe of the approach slab.

A second way to find the Round Room, and perhaps the easiest way, is to stay on the dirt service road that loops around West Mountain's south end. This road is more distant from the mountain than the trails mentioned above. From the point on this road 30 yards south of West Mountain's southernmost boulder, walk east, then northeast on this road. A wash will be to your left. After 175 yards you should see a pile of dozens of football to basketball size rocks on your left (northwest) placed there to prevent the road from eroding into the wash. 15 feet west of this pile is a 10 foot tall mesquite on the northwest side of the road. Behind the pile of rocks is an 8 foot wide notch

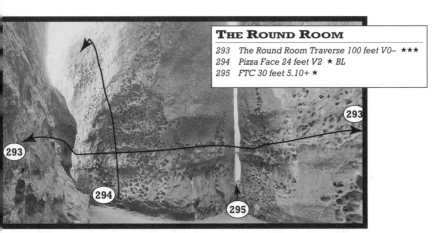

THE ROUND ROOM

293 The Round Room Traverse 100 feet V0– ★★★
294 Pizza Face 24 feet V2 ★ BL
295 FTC 30 feet 5.10+ ★

dropping into the wash. Directly across the wash from this notch is an 8 foot wide trail (formerly a dirt road) that leads to the approach slab (the black water streak mentioned above can be seen at the northwest end of this wide trail).

293 The Round Room Traverse 100 feet V0– ★★★ Only in Hueco Tanks. Traverse the entire room in either direction.

Variation 1: Pursuit Race-2 climbers start on opposite sides and chase each other until one is caught or someone falls.

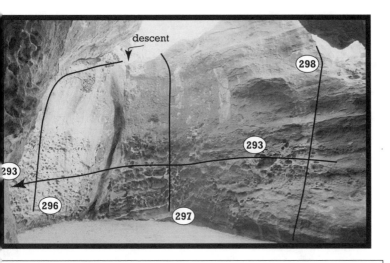

THE ROUND ROOM

293 The Round Room Traverse 100 feet V0– ★★★   297 Loose Screw 24 feet V1 ★ BL
296 The Unnameable 25 feet V3 ★★ scary   298 STB 20 feet V0+

Variation 2: Time Trial-Record attempts are timed starting on the right side of the slabby South Face wall and ending 100 feet later at the same point. This has been done in under 40 seconds.

Variation 3: Tag-Play tag, but stay on the walls.

Warning: Partiers sometimes throw bottles against the walls. Look out for glass in the huecos.

294　**Pizza Face 24 feet V2 ★ BL** Instead of pulling the hideously loose lip off, stem behind you at the top to back off.

295　**FTC 30 feet 5.10+ ★** Offwidth until you can squeeze through the chimney at the top.

296　**The Unnameable 25 feet V3 ★★ scary**

297　**Loose Screw 24 feet V1 ★ BL scary loose** The last 6 feet are the crux. There's a ¼ inch stud above the lip on this. A bad landing if one doesn't fall far enough out from the wall to miss the base.

298　**STB 20 feet V0+** Avoid an early exit to the right.

THE NORWEGIAN WALL

This is a magnificent long jug traverse wall guaranteed to pump even the burliest arms. A 15-foot diameter natural arch near the top end of the wall (hard to see from ground level) provides a distinctive finish to one of the problems. To find the wall go 180 yards south of the pass between East and West Mountain to the curve in the sandy dirt service road that winds between East Spur and West Mountain. A rusted white trash barrel usually sits 15 yards

NORWEGIAN WALL, BETWEEN THE SHEETS WITH APPROACHES

Norwegian Wall

Between the Sheets

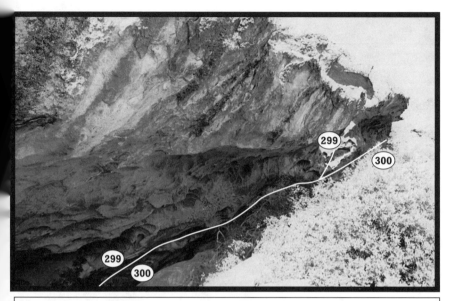

NORWEGIAN WALL

299   Between the Shits 45 feet V5 ★★★
300   Corey The Pimp 105 feet V9 ★★★

north of this curve. Ascend the slabs to the west for 200 yards to the wall. The landings are bad in places, but these problems are relatively safe with a good spotter. Twenty and 30 yards uphill from the arch are two large boulders leaning against the wall. To descend, downclimb the wall above the uphill boulder, then downclimb that boulder. Beware of loose rock on the downclimb.

299   **Between the Shits 45 feet V5 ★★★** Start in a deep two-hand undercling slot. Climb out then right and exit through the natural arch.

300   **Corey The Pimp 105 feet V9 ★★★** Climb Between The Shits, then instead of exiting through the arch, keep traversing 60 feet and top the wall out just before a boulder blocks the way. Sixty additional feet of traversing moves, dubbed Abs of Steel, have been done left of Between the Shits, but have yet to be linked to that problem or Corey The Pimp.

301   **Norbat 23 feet V7 ★★** This problem climbs the right side of the thick rib on the overhang behind the descent boulder, exiting just left of that boulder. The left side of the rib has been attempted and would top out at the same place.

NORWEGIAN WALL

301   **Norbat 23 feet V7** ★★

BETWEEN THE SHEETS

The photo on page 66 shows the approach to the following problems. The approach starts on the first major tongue of rock 75 yards southwest of Tlaloc Pass (the pass between East and West Mountains). A major fissure system runs 270 yards up this tongue to Between The Sheets (BTS). Down low on the tongue, this fissure system forms a long north-facing overhang with several loose hold, bad landing problems. At Between The Sheets, the fissure is parallel sided and only 3 to 4 feet wide.

302   **Between The Cheeks 25 feet V7** ★★★ **SD** Same start as Between The Sheets.

303   **Between The Sheets 20 feet V4** ★★★ **SD** Start crouched down with both hands jammed in the horizontal crack at the roof's base.

304   **Between The Puffs 19 feet V5** ★★ **SD**

There are several easier lines to the right of Between the Sheets.

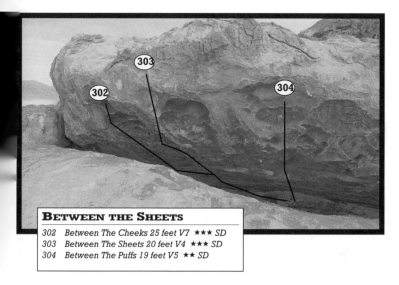

BETWEEN THE SHEETS

302	Between The Cheeks 25 feet V7 ★★★ SD
303	Between The Sheets 20 feet V4 ★★★ SD
304	Between The Puffs 19 feet V5 ★★ SD

SECRET SHARER AREA

BIKO ROCK

This is the 50 foot tall, roof-capped north-facing rock directly above Green Blanket Buttress (Secret Sharer). The easiest approach is to walk up a hidden ramp system to the right of The Pit Roof. Diagonal left up this ramp over the top of The Pit Roof, threading your way through boulders and trees to the base of Biko Rock. Alternately, approach up easy 5th class terrain left of Green Blanket Buttress.

Biko Rock

NORTH SIDE OF WEST MOUNTAIN FROM MAIN DAM

Pit Roof

Secret Sharer

BIKO ROCK

305	*Creatures of the New Left 55 feet 5.10* ★★
306	*Biko Roof 45 feet 5.12*
307	*Wet Blanket Face 40 feet 5.10- TR* ★
308	*Green Blanket Crack 40 fee t 5.10-*
309	*The Secret Sharer 45 feet 5.12-* ★★★

305   Creatures of the New Left 55 feet 5.10 ★★   1 bolt.

306   Biko Roof 45 feet 5.12   4 bolts.

GREEN BLANKET BUTTRESS

This 45-foot ship's prow buttress is located at ground level below Biko Rock, on the south side of The Pit, 185 yards east from the south end of the main dam.

307   **Wet Blanket Face 40 feet 5.10– TR** ★   The face 7 feet left of Green Blanket Crack.

308   **Green Blanket Crack 40 feet 5.10–**

309   **The Secret Sharer 45 feet 5.12–** ★★★   4 bolts, 2 bolt anchor.

     Variation: From half height move right and finish up left side of arete (5.12 TR).

INDEX

This is an index of named routes and features only. Formations of areas are in all capitals.